3808

FGEN (Don)

D0735182

THE OECD
DECLARATION AND DECISIONS
ON INTERNATIONAL INVESTMENT
AND MULTINATIONAL ENTERPRISES

1991 REVIEW

ORGANISATION FOR ECONOMIC CO-OPERATION AND DEVELOPMENT

ORGANISATION FOR ECONOMIC CO-OPERATION AND DEVELOPMENT

Pursuant to Article 1 of the Convention signed in Paris on 14th December 1960, and which came into force on 30th September 1961, the Organisation for Economic Co-operation and Development (OECD) shall promote policies designed:

— to achieve the highest sustainable economic growth and employment and a rising standard of living in Member countries, while maintaining financial stability, and thus to contribute to the development of the world economy;

— to contribute to sound economic expansion in Member as well as non-member countries in the process of economic development; and

— to contribute to the expansion of world trade on a multilateral, non-discriminatory basis in accordance with international obligations.

The original Member countries of the OECD are Austria, Belgium, Canada, Denmark, France, Germany, Greece, Iceland, Ireland, Italy, Luxembourg, the Netherlands, Norway, Portugal, Spain, Sweden, Switzerland, Turkey, the United Kingdom and the United States. The following countries became Members subsequently through accession at the dates indicated hereafter: Japan (28th April 1964), Finland (28th January 1969), Australia (7th June 1971) and New Zealand (29th May 1973). The Commission of the European Communities takes part in the work of the OECD (Article 13 of the OECD Convention). Yugoslavia has a special status at OECD (agreement of 28th October 1961).

HG
4538
.O33
1992

Publié en français sous le titre :

LA DÉCLARATION ET LES DÉCISIONS DE L'OCDE
SUR L'INVESTISSEMENT INTERNATIONAL
ET LES ENTREPRISES MULTINATIONALES :
examen 1991

FOREWORD

OECD fosters a favourable investment environment by promoting international co-operation among its Member countries. This co-operation operates primarily in the framework of the OECD Declaration and Decisions on International Investment and Multinational Enterprises which covers four broad areas: National Treatment of established foreign-controlled enterprises, Guidelines for Multinational Enterprises (MNEs), and co-operation regarding Conflicting Requirements imposed on MNEs by Governments in different countries and International Investment Incentives and Disincentives.

The 1991 Review of the OECD Declaration and Decisions on International Investments and Multinational Enterprises examines experience in applying these instruments over the past seven years and reports on the ways they have been strengthened. It also provides an analysis of recent trends in international direct investment flows.

This Report has been prepared by the Committee on International Investment and Multinational Enterprises in accordance with the requirements of the Declaration and Decisions mentioned above. It was approved by the Committee in September 1991 and derestricted by the Council in December 1991.

ALSO AVAILABLE

CONTENTS

Chapter I

THE CLIMATE FOR INTERNATIONAL DIRECT INVESTMENT

Over the last fifty years, international direct investment has been a major force in shaping the development of the world economy. This was particularly true in the 1980s when, after a period of weakness early in the decade, annual direct investment flows rose fourfold to unprecedented levels. Increasing numbers of the most dynamic industries and firms take part in this move towards internationalisation, and more and more countries are involved, both as home and host countries.

The Review period (1984-91) has been one of generally strong economic growth in the OECD area after a long and difficult period of slow growth and structural adjustment. While the recovery did not involve the entire world economy – Latin America and Africa being largely left aside – this recovery has encompassed the whole of the OECD area and certain parts of the developing world, particularly the Dynamic Asian Economies (DAEs)[1]. Throughout the period, countries have developed greater interdependence in a world marked by increasing economic and financial integration, while business has become even more international, with increasing numbers of companies adopting a global approach in outlook, strategy and operation. Internationalisation and the rapid growth of foreign direct investment have been aided by a widespread trend towards the liberalisation of policies towards international direct investment. This trend which has not been confined to the OECD area has often been associated with broad-based structural reforms designed to stimulate economic activity by creating a more propitious investment environment.

Many non-Member countries, however, face a harsh economic environment that is not conducive to encouraging much needed foreign direct investment. Growth rates have been low and external debt a continuing burden. Domestic economic reforms accompanied by debt relief in various forms have improved the situation in some cases, but overall achievements have been modest and the outlook remains worrying, especially in Africa. This rather bleak picture is in sharp contrast to the spectacular achievements of the DAEs where rapid economic growth has attracted very substantial direct investments that have stimulated further growth. The economic success of these countries is such that some of them have become significant exporters of direct investment, especially to neighbouring areas less advanced than themselves.

Radical reforms are being undertaken in the countries of central and eastern Europe where foreign investment has a major role to play in the challenging transition to a market economy. These economies are now experiencing difficult transitional problems, including acute stabilisation difficulties and longer term problems of adjustment to a market economy. Previous trade patterns have been disturbed, there is a foreign debt overhang, undetermined environmental responsibilities and unanswered questions of ownership. Social and political tensions have arisen as a result of declining real wages, rising unemployment and the closure of uneconomic enterprises. Nevertheless, important progress has already been achieved in Poland, Hungary and the Czech and Slovak Federal Republic (CSFR). Budget deficits have been reduced, subsidies are being cut, interest rates are positive and the monetary overhang has been reduced. These countries demonstrate a strong commitment to reform, and some have taken important steps to liberalise the regimes governing private enterprise and foreign direct investment which has a crucial role to play in the reform process. Foreign investment brings much needed capital, technology and management skills and contributes to exports of a quality that is competitive on world markets. It is also a significant element in privatisation programmes and a means of exposing domestic enterprises to competitive world market forces.

In the course of the 1980s, the international economy has shown a notable degree of strength and resilience through a period marked by continued large external imbalances and high indebtedness, major exchange rate movements and stock market instability. Of particular note, despite these difficulties, has been the strength with which international co-operation and disciplines have been maintained and even developed. Among these, the OECD instruments related to international direct investment have figured prominently, serving to maintain an open international economic system and to improve the climate for international direct investment. Non-Member countries, moreover, are increasingly coming to appreciate the need to improve the climate for foreign direct investment and are taking steps to adjust their policies in this direction.

Recently, however, there have been a number of signs of a resurgence of protectionist pressures. Consolidation of these pressures and their embodiment in laws, regulations or government practices would not only endanger the progress achieved but would also represent a major threat to the open multilateral system that has served the world economy so well. OECD countries have a special responsibility in this regard. They need to act, individually and collectively, to preserve an open, non-discriminatory regime for international direct investment in the best interests of all countries.

The present chapter reviews the climate for international direct investment over the period 1984-91, including trends in international direct investment for the OECD area as well as for non-Member countries; trends in policies towards direct investment; and the role of the OECD instruments which are aimed at increasing international co-operation in the field of international investment and multinational enterprises.

1. Recent trends in international direct investment

In the years of uninterrupted growth of the 1950s and 1960s, international direct investment flows grew at a rate approximately twice the rate of growth of the world economy. It is more difficult, however, to reach straightforward conclusions for the 1970s and 1980s because of difficulties of statistical measurement. One difficulty is that countries differ in their treatment of reinvested earnings, which have taken on greater importance in recent years. Another derives from the fluctuations in intra-company transactions (especially lending) and the role of tax-havens and offshore banking centres. Exchange rate changes, too, have important effects on international direct investment statistics because of their impact on the valuation of stocks and flows when converted to a common currency. The OECD, with the publication in 1982 of the *Detailed Benchmark*

8

Definition of Foreign Direct Investment, has been taking steps to improve the methodology and comparability of direct investment statistics. These efforts are continuing with the publication, in 1992, of a revised version of the Benchmark Definition, which is designed to bring the methodology more closely into line with the present reality of direct investment transactions.

Despite the methodological difficulties it can be clearly stated that the rate of growth of direct investment in the 70s and the 80s has still been higher than that of the world economy or that of domestic investment and that overall, average annual outward investment flows over the 80s (in nominal, dollar terms) are about double their level of the 70s. The strong and uninterrupted growth of foreign direct investment over the review period has also been associated with important changes in the geographical patterns of direct investment flows. These and other key features of foreign direct investment patterns are highlighted below.

The OECD area

A number of notable developments are evident in recent trends in international direct investment in the OECD area. First of these is the very strong growth of outward investment after a fall-off in the early 80s. From a 1982 low of $24 billion, outward investment, particularly since 1984, has achieved year-on-year increases averaging 30 per cent, with 1988 and 1989 levels reaching $154 billion and $174 billion respectively. Another important feature, as seen from Tables 1 and 2 is the growing involvement of more and more countries as both home and host countries to international direct investment. Traditional roles as source or host countries in the 70s are now more blurred as international direct investment has become more widespread and diverse. As a result of their dual roles more countries have now a greater and more balanced stake in international direct investment.

Japan, the United Kingdom and the United States have been the leading sources of outward investment over the Review period, each registering around 20 per cent of total outward flows over the period 1985-1989. Japanese investment abroad has expanded strongly, particularly since 1986, and Japan was the single largest source of foreign direct investment in 1989, accounting for 25 per cent of total outflows that year. The UK situation, following major expansion in 1986/7 has stabilised at around $33 billion over the last three years. For the United States, there was an unusual period in the early 80s when outflows were very low, but these picked up sharply after 1984, with 1989 outflows at around $32 billion, 18 per cent of the total. Particular mention may also be made of investments from EFTA countries, which have expanded fourfold since 1984, mainly accounted for by new investments in countries of the European Community.

A major feature of the Review period has been the very considerable expansion of inward investment into the United States which has received over half of total OECD inflows in the 1985-1989 period. Trends in inward investment into the United States are explained first and foremost by the strong growth of its large, unified market. Investors have also sought to benefit from technologies developed in the United States, while major restructuring of US companies has given many foreign investors access to the US market through acquisitions. In fact, the growth of foreign acquisitions has been one of the key features of inward investment in the United States. Throughout the 80s, acquisitions have exceeded new establishments (in value terms), but the proportion of acquisitions to total inward investments has grown from 67 per cent in the first half of the 80s to 87 per cent

9

Table 1. Outward direct investment flows

US $ million

Based on Balance of Payments Data

Countries	Cumulative flows of direct investment		Flows of direct investment								
	1971-1980	1981-1989	1981	1982	1983	1984	1985	1986	1987	1988	1989¹
Australia	2 510	23 222	734	693	518	1 403	1 660	2 992	5 733	5 720	3 769
Austria	578	2 447	206	150	186	67	49	296	347	287	859
BLEU*	3 213	2 222	30	-77	358	282	231	1 627	2 680	3 609	-6 518
Canada	11 335	35 047	5 756	709	2 758	2 277	2 855	4 066	6 546	5 943	4 137
Denmark	1 063	476	141	77	159	93	303	646	618	719	2 027
Finland	605	7 957	147	240	269	423	350	752	895	1 969	2 912
France*	13 940	58 624	4 615	3 063	1 841	2 126	2 226	5 230	8 704	12 756	18 063
Germany*	23 130	62 168	3 862	2 481	3 170	4 389	4 804	9 616	9 105	11 286	13 455
Italy*	3 597	20 808	1 404	1 025	2 126	1 995	1 818	2 661	2 326	5 450	2 003
Japan*	18 052	137 802	4 894	4 540	3 612	5 965	6 452	14 480	19 519	34 210	44 130
Netherlands*	27 829	38 763	3 629	2 610	2 098	2 531	2 829	3 182	7 120	4 090	10 674
Norway*	1 079	7 066	185	317	360	612	1 228	1 605	890	505	1 364
Portugal²	38	202	20	10	18	10	22	0	-10	56	76
Spain	1 274	5 351	272	505	245	249	252	377	754	1 227	1 470
Sweden	4 597	23 962	854	985	1 056	1 049	1 273	3 062	3 175	5 298	7 210
Switzerland		24 580			492	1 139	4 572	1 461	1 274	8 696	6 946
United Kingdom	55 112	163 427	12 065	7 145	8 211	8 027	10 851	17 269	31 391	36 774	31 675
United States³	134 354	139 699	9 624	967	6 695	11 587	13 162	18 679	31 045	16 218	31 722
Total	302 306	753 823	48 438	25 440	34 172	44 224	54 937	88 001	132 112	154 813	175 974

1. Revised figures.
2. 1975-80.
3. United States figures have now been revised to exclude capital gains and losses, bringing them into line with the figures provided for other Member countries.
* These countries do not include reinvested earnings in their foreign direct investment statistics.
Source: ESD/DAFFE, OECD, January 1991.

Table 2. Inward direct investment flows

US$ million

Based on Balance of Payments Data

Countries	Cumulative flows of direct investment		Flows of direct investment								
	1971-1980	1981-1989	1981	1982	1983	1984	1985	1986	1987	1988	1989[1]
Australia	11 295	31 638	2 254	2 232	2 994	428	2 086	3 273	3 656	7 175	7 540
Austria	1 455	2 648	318	206	220	117	168	182	403	444	590
BLEU*	9 215	20 000	1 352	1 390	1 271	360	957	631	2 338	4 990	6 711
Canada	5 534	6 084	-3 670	-831	243	1 313	-2 050	990	3 319	3 898	2 872
Denmark	1 561	308	100	135	64	9	109	161	88	504	1 084
Finland	376	1 147	17	-14	16	54	63	321	96	278	316
France*	16 908	34 154	2 426	1 563	1 631	2 198	2 210	2 749	4 621	7 204	9 552
Germany*	13 957	14 467	340	819	1 775	553	587	1 190	1 901	1 369	5 933
Greece		5 140	520	436	439	485	447	471	683	907	752
Ireland	1 659	1 113	204	241	168	119	159	-43	89	91	85
Italy*	5 698	18 677	1 146	636	1 190	1 290	1 003	-15	4 059	6 839	2 529
Japan*	1 424	1 528	189	439	416	-10	642	226	1 165	-485	-1 054
Netherlands*	10 822	18 383	1 520	934	757	587	641	1 897	2 313	4 042	5 692
Norway[2]	3 074	3 670	686	424	336	-210	-412	1 023	184	271	1 368
Portugal[2]	535	3 975	177	145	144	196	254	242	317	877	1 623
Spain	7 060	32 319	1 714	1 801	1 647	1 773	1 945	3 442	4 548	7 016	8 433
Sweden	897	3 893	182	185	55	156	270	825	339	886	995
Switzerland		7 617			286	520	1 050	1 778	2 044	42	1 897
United Kingdom	40 503	88 935	5 891	5 286	5 132	-241	4 960	7 311	14 194	16 397	30 004
United States[3]	56 276	306 979	25 195	13 792	11 946	25 359	19 022	34 091	46 894	58 436	72 244
Total	188 249	602 675	40 561	29 819	30 730	35 056	34 111	60 745	93 251	121 181	159 166

1. Revised figures.
2. 1975-80.
3. United States figures have now been revised to exclude capital gains and losses, bringing them into line with the figures provided for other Member countries.
* These countries do not include reinvested earnings in their foreign direct investment statistics.
Source: ESD/DAFFE, OECD, January 1991

11

in the latter half. An interesting feature is the growing size of these acquisitions; in 1988, twelve acquisitions were in excess of $1 billion, and five of these exceeded $2 billion. Around 75 per cent of the foreign acquisitions over the period since 1984 have been made by the already established affiliates of foreign companies in the United States, as opposed to non-resident investors, a share that has changed little over the 80s. This acquisition activity over the review period is related to corporate restructuring in US companies, which involved the shedding of unprofitable activities outside their main lines of business, the desire by foreign multinationals to acquire US companies to round out their global market position and the availability of funds to do so.

Europe has moved from being the premier host region to international direct investment in the 70s to becoming also a major source in the 1980s. Outward investment from the United Kingdom, but also Germany, France and the Netherlands has expanded considerably, with the United States being the single largest destination; the growth of investment flows from France since the mid-1980s has been quite spectacular. Inward investment into European countries has been prompted by renewed economic growth, the accession of Spain and Portugal to the European Community and the pursuit of more welcoming policies towards foreign investment. In addition, many investments, both from within and outside the Community, are being made in anticipation of the single European market of 1992. Financial market deregulation and the "Big Bang" in London and other international financial centres provided financing for international direct investment and stimulated investments in the financial services industry. The combined effect of these various factors is reflected in the variety of the sources of investment into the EC, particularly since 1987. Intra-Community, US and Japanese investments have been important, while in recent years investment from the EFTA area has exceeded that from the United States and Japan.

Japanese investment abroad, which grew steadily in the first half of the 1980s, has undergone a veritable explosion since 1985, placing Japan together with the United States and the United Kingdom in the group of the three principal source countries. In fact, Japan was, in 1989, the largest single source country, its $44 billion accounting for around one-quarter of total outward investment from the OECD area. The strength of the Japanese economy and its external surplus, appreciation of the yen and globalisation of Japanese firms' strategies are important forces behind this surge. The characteristics of Japanese outward investment have also been changing, moving distinctly away from labour intensive to processing and assembly industries, technology intensive industries and, especially in Europe, in the area of banking and financial services including insurance. Inward investment into Japan is still very modest, particularly in comparison to outward investment levels. The growth of the Japanese market presents a strong attraction to foreign investors and Japan's laws and regulations covering international direct investment are quite liberal. Nevertheless, it seems that the complexity of doing business in Japan, together with the relative lack of acquisition opportunities, remain important forces leading to low inward investment levels.

At the sectoral level, and while investment in manufacturing continues to be important, a major trend over the 1980s has been the growth of foreign direct investment in the services sector. The most important areas have been finance and trade-related services, although investment in accounting, advertising and transport has also been sizeable. One reason behind the increasing importance of direct investment in the services sector is the growing internationalisation of service corporations. Another factor is the liberalisation and deregulation of important service sector activities, coupled with the internationalisation of financial markets and the diversification of financial instruments.

Non-Member countries

The harsh economic situation facing many non-Member countries has taken its toll on international direct investment, where many countries' inward investment has been flat or in decline, particularly in Africa and the major Latin American countries with high levels of indebtedness. As shown in Table 3, inward investment to non-Member countries as a whole did not catch up with the 1981 peak of $17 billion until 1987. Since 1987, there has been a renewed rise in international direct investment to those countries, most of this being attributable to higher Japanese investment in Asia and flows to the Latin American offshore banking centres. Only a few of the more developed countries, especially in South East Asia, have attracted increasing amounts of international direct investment. The present situation, where non-Member countries are receiving a falling share of direct investment flows is in sharp contrast to that of the second half of the 70s, when these countries experienced considerable growth of such flows (see table 4).

The situation facing many non-Member countries is still difficult. Higher levels of international direct investment would be particularly useful in respect of debt and structural adjustment, but only some of them have benefited from significant direct investment flows. Moreover, their prospects for attracting foreign investment must be set in the context of concerns with a world "capital shortage". OECD savings performance has declined, and coupled with rising investment demand over the 1980s, this has brought pressures on real interest rates, which have remained at historically high levels throughout the OECD recovery. In the highly indebted countries, concrete progress with the adoption of "menu" options including debt and debt service reduction and the provision of new funds along the lines proposed in the Brady initiative provide the basis for the adoption of sounder policies that would encourage new investment flows. The clear implication is that capital will have to be allocated more efficiently.

Foreign investment in Central and Eastern Europe has so far been relatively unimportant, mainly taking the form of joint ventures and quasi-investment arrangements, such as some buy-back operations, co-production agreements and leasing arrangements. Foreign investment with full or majority foreign participation has not been significant but can be expected to expand as a result of recent important changes in legislation. In the longer term, prospects for foreign direct investment in Central and Eastern Europe are more promising. The potential market is very large and the proximity of the region to western European markets coupled with relatively low labour costs will provide incentives for direct investment geared to both local and export production. There are important opportunities for developing new products and updating outmoded technology. In the short term, however, the political and economic uncertainties and risks of stabilisation and transition, the inadequacy of basic infrastructure, the debt burden and, the lack of clarity in the regimes governing intellectual property rights, access to foreign exchange and foreign remittances, and the absence of a legal framework specifying clearly and fully the rights and obligations of foreign investors explain why potential foreign investors are still adopting a cautious approach to investment in this area for the time being.

Table 3. **Total net resource flows to developing countries**

Current $ billion

	1980	1981	1982	1983	1984	1985	1986	1987	1988	1989
I. Official development finance (ODF)	45.6	45.5	44.2	42.4	47.7	48.9	56.2	61.6	66.1	67.1
II. Total export credits	16.5	17.6	13.7	4.6	6.2	4.0	-0.7	-2.6	-0.5	1.2
III. Private flows	66.2	74.3	58.2	47.9	31.7	31.4	28.2	34.4	38.7	40.7
of which:										
1. Direct investment (OECD)[1]	11.2(16.9)	17.2(23.0)	12.8(21.0)	9.3(19.3)	11.3(35.6)	6.6(21.4)	11.3(40.1)	20.9(56.7)	23.4(57.8)	22.0(54.0)
2. International bank lending	49.0	52.3	37.9	35.0	17.2	15.2	7.0	7.0	5.8	8.5
Total net resource flows (I + II + III)	128.3	137.4	116.1	94.9	85.6	84.3	83.7	93.4	104.3	109.0

1. Figures in parenthesis are share of direct investment to total private resource flows.
Source: Financing and External Debt of Developing Countries OECD 1990.

Table 4. **International Direct Investment in Developing Countries by DAC countries ($ million) 1976-1988**[1]

	Cumulative Flows				Flows								
	1976/83	%[2]	1984/89	%[2]	1981	1982	1983	1984	1985	1986	1987	1988	1989
LATIN AMERICA	43 822	47.5	52 462	50.1	6 235	5 898	3 817	5 810	5 091	6 289	10 560	12 855	11 857
of which off-shore centres[3]	6 973		29 290		1 760	2 776	2 437	2 350	3 284	4 255	8 264	6 813	4 324
Mexico	3 604		3 786		1 226	-1 038	-325	580	359	-9	546	812	1 498
Argentina	3 434		949		580	379	105	135	172	348	217	-39	116
Brazil	10 350		9 574		1 349	1 610	674	1 477	550	564	1 380	2 729	2 874
ASIA	23 998	26.0	33 732	32.2	6 505	2 459	3 412	4 688	656	3 026	8 212	7 797	9 353
Hong Kong	3 590		8 903		1 088	652	603	679	-142	996	3 298	2 675	1 397
Indonesia	4 439		338		2 584	537	303	494	-311	-581	-570	-14	1 320
Korea	394		2 706		261	107	-62	246	169	370	828	754	339
Malaysia	57		2 005		252	-429	234	227	140	-32	384	674	612
Singapore	2 982		6 017		980	280	418	865	252	603	930	1 678	1 689
Taiwan	590		2 256		119	57	120	208	110	278	766	186	708
Thailand	902		2 496		219	128	200	348	-98	-5	441	513	1 297
Philippines	944		602		115	126	-168	167	-250	60	78	215	332
AFRICA	11 341	12.3	4 046	3.9	1 983	2 448	978	-36	491	485	444	1 223	1 439
North Sahara	2 107		1 292		153	160	606	249	789	-181	-83	264	254
South Sahara	7 563		2 909		1 809	2 239	337	-230	-218	613	1 174	520	1 110
Total Developing Countries	92 310		104 613		16 851	12 358	9 127	11 137	6 442	11 146	20 882	24 959	30 047

1. Some figures include reinvested earnings, others do not, and some also include oil.
2. Share of developing countries' total.
3. Latin American offshore centres: The Bahamas, Barbados, Bermuda, the Cayman Islands, the Netherlands Antilles, Panama, St Lucia and the Virgin Islands.
Source: Geographical distribution of financial flows to developing countries, OECD.

2. The policy environment and international direct investment

The OECD area

Questions concerning international direct investment and foreign ownership and control had already been raised in the mid-60s in the OECD area, notably in connection with the first major waves of the expansion of US-based firms abroad. But the experience of the late 60s and early 70s and especially the insufficient level of domestic investment since the mid-70s turned attention to the positive contributions that international direct investment offers in terms of employment, technology, competition, managerial techniques and so on. From then on, liberalisation gained impetus and has continued and developed to the present. These efforts have been part and parcel of a broader trend in the OECD area encompassing liberalisation of cross-border capital and service operations, greater recourse to the operation of market forces, deregulation and privatisation, fiscal reform and so on.

The generally more welcoming attitude to international direct investment in the OECD area is also related to the growing internationalisation and interdependence of economies, with more and more companies looking beyond their borders for investment, technology and market opportunities. Also, as countries increasingly play a dual role as both host and home countries to international direct investment, they have taken a more balanced involvement in the process. Equally, international direct investment has achieved a certain maturity and countries have gained in experience with it, realising that multinational enterprises are generally good corporate citizens, concerned with their image and wishing to be integrated into the domestic environment. Their performance in host countries, over good and rough periods, has broadly been at least on a par with domestic enterprises, as shown by the Committee's study on *Structural Adjustment and Multinational Enterprises,* published in 1985. All in all, OECD countries now feel much more comfortable with international direct investment and multinational enterprises. Accordingly, in countries where the policy framework had been based on controlling and ensuring benefits via restrictions and conditions, the emphasis is now on attracting international direct investment by reducing obstacles and impediments as far as possible.

The result has been a major improvement in the overall climate for international direct investment in the OECD area. Countries still have certain measures related to inward direct investment. These tend to be taken for specific reasons, such as to protect essential security interests or cultural identity. Even the most liberal countries have some sector-specific measures, which tend to be concentrated in the areas of natural resources and services (particularly transport, communications and insurance) with notably few in the manufacturing sector. Where measures do exist, the objective is not so much to prevent international direct investment as to pursue a cautious approach to opening up areas to foreign investors by controlling the pace of their entry. As the record has shown, growing liberalisation and higher inward investment levels have had strong interactive effects, to the clear benefit of the OECD area. International direct investment is now generally welcome throughout the OECD area, and even where screening procedures remain, genuine investments are not often refused.

In Yugoslavia, which is a "special status" country in the OECD, a regulatory reform of direct investment has the objective of bringing that regime into closer conformity with the direct investment regimes of OECD countries. In that sense, the Foreign Investment Law, which came into force in the beginning of 1989, provides that foreign investors can hold majority shares as well as full ownership in enterprises in many economic sectors. Foreign fully-owned enterprises have the same status and rights as domestic enterprises.

Investment policies in non-Member countries

Throughout the 1970s, many non-Member countries were suspicious of international direct investment. Some were hostile to foreign ownership and control per se, for reasons of economic nationalism and sovereignty in respect of particular, key sectors such as natural resources. In other cases, the concerns lay more with the contribution of international direct investment to development, with a view that the gains were skewed in favour of multinational enterprises. Specific issues lay with the extent to which capital inflows were spent on imports (rather than locally produced inputs), a perceived lack of technology transfer, excessive financial transfers and a feeling that multinational enterprises were lacking in commitment to the host country. The result was a long list of restrictions, including outright bans (particularly in certain sectors), authorisation procedures, foreign ownership ceilings, repatriation restrictions, conditions stipulating technology transfer, local content and export requirements and so on. In many cases, these measures were combined with investment incentives (including trade protection measures) to offset costs imposed by restrictions or conditions, but the result was often the reverse of that intended – inefficient operations, poor international competitiveness, limited contribution to exports. In some cases, policies were self-defeating – conditions were imposed to increase or ensure certain benefits, but these were so onerous or unacceptable that investors turned elsewhere as shown, for example, in the Committee's study *Investment Incentives and Disincentives: Effects on International Direct Investment,* published in 1989. Overall, there is likely to have been considerable distortion to both investment and trade flows. Yet despite this, developing countries still achieved growing levels of inward investment, in some cases, because of liberal approaches geared to export promotion and in other, more restrictive countries due to protection and incentives geared to import substitution and the domestic market.

At a time when more international direct investment is wanted by developing countries, however, the trend in many cases has been downward or has shown signs of improvement only since the late 1980's. Changing attitudes have led to some policy changes in the direction of liberalisation, but in much of Latin America and Africa, moves have often been confused and dispersed and the positive developments in a number of countries need to be consolidated. The situation of the DAEs has been more favourable and, indeed, these countries generally are emerging as both host and home countries to international direct investment. This, together with their technological position, presents them with opportunities to assume greater responsibilities in promoting an open investment climate.

While signs of a clear and sustained upswing of international direct investment in non-Member countries are still fragmentary, there is a more receptive attitude to such investment along with policies geared to the domestic economic scene and to the market mechanism and private investment in general. Such moves, including privatisation will, if successful, improve the economic climate which would encourage international direct investment. There is, therefore, a very crucial task in the years ahead for international co-operation to develop and apply multilateral rules of the game and their associated disciplines to improve the climate for international direct investment and the contribution it can make to sustainable development.

Beginning around 1986, but especially since 1989, there have been a number of important developments in central and eastern European countries' legislation on foreign investment, covering both joint ventures as well as majority or full foreign participations. This has been the case particularly in Hungary, Poland and the CSFR, but also in the Soviet Union, with the objective of making the conditions under which these operate more attractive to Western investors. New legislation to facilitate joint ventures has been introduced, and since the beginning of 1989, foreign investors may hold a majority or exclusive stake in most of the countries of the region. This being said, it is likely that there is still a preference on the part of the authorities for joint ventures, which are seen as having an important role to play in restructuring, technology transfer and improving management practices and training. The situation with respect to the purchase of domestic companies and the extent to which foreign investors may face restrictions in acquiring firms to be privatised is also often unclear. Where this is permitted, for example in Poland, applications will be treated on a case-by-case basis, given the concern that foreign companies may buy up the most promising firms during the period when domestic financial resources are limited. Other difficulties include the uncertainty of establishing property ownership, the valuation of existing businesses and the effects of past policy failures on health and the environment. Finally, it should also be noted that there is a greater willingness and readiness to conclude bilateral investment protection agreements, although there are still difficult issues to be resolved in negotiating the elements of such agreements.

While many of the reforms mentioned above are relatively recent, it is clear that there has been an acceleration and widening of moves towards economic reform, covering more countries and more facets of economic behaviour. To the extent that these moves become more concrete and established and that the traditional problems of conducting business in these countries can be overcome, this will open up important economic opportunities for foreign investors and create a new role for foreign direct investment in the countries concerned.

Emerging concerns

While liberalisation momentum has built up and spread in the OECD area, recent years have seen a number of signs in policies and practices counter to this liberalisation trend. If such moves broaden and strengthen, there is a very real and serious danger that they may awaken latent parallel pressures in other countries in retaliation and result in a significant deterioration in the climate for international direct investment. This section examines these areas of concern, why they have arisen and what might be done to halt them.

One of the principal causes of present investment protectionist pressures is that trade frictions have been overflowing into the investment area. For example, the United States 1988 Omnibus Trade and Competitiveness Act contained in its earlier drafts a number of disturbing provisions related to international direct investment, which were strongly opposed by the United States Administration. The final version of the Act does go some way to providing reassurance that the United States' open investment regime will be maintained. However, concerns remain particularly in respect of the ''Exon-Florio'' provisions related to foreign acquisitions and national security, because of uncertainty about the range of activities that may be covered by the provisions and the manner in which regulations may be implemented. The US authorities have indicated the Exon-Florio provisions should not be seen as a screening mechanism and that the President's new authority to block individual foreign investments for national security reasons may be used only when there is clear evidence of a threat to national security and when other, existing provisions are not able or suitable to deal with the matter. While the US Administration has reviewed over 500 investments since the passage of Exon-Florio, it has blocked only one transaction.

More generally, provisions maintained by OECD governments based on essential security and public order considerations have remained relatively extensive and in some cases they have been extended. Efforts are underway in the Organisation to limit the use of such measures to areas where these concerns are clearly predominant and to bring these measures more fully under international surveillance.

Another concern is found in the case of so-called "screwdriver" plants in Europe where it is felt that assembly and low value-added international direct investment is sometimes being used to circumvent anti-dumping trade single measures. Other frictions with implications for direct investment have arisen from the debates on local content requirements in respect of some European countries and also in relation to rules of origin in connection with the free circulation of goods in the European Community.

Changes in the pattern of international direct investment flows also play a role. In the United States, for example, as was the case in Europe in the mid-60s, the strong upsurge of inward investment has resulted in public discussion of the possible threat to the national economic interest of sharply increased foreign ownership and penetration, including the possible threat to national security of international direct investment in defence and related sensitive areas. Some similar pressures are also found in other countries, most notably in respect of foreign acquisitions of well known domestic companies. In some cases, such concerns are directed at foreign investment in general, in others more to such investment from specific countries or areas.

Moves towards the single European market in 1992 are already promoting more liberal investment regimes within the EC and encouraging direct investment by creating a large and more unified market. However, concerns have been expressed about the treatment of non-EC enterprises. One of the key issues relates to the requirement of reciprocity in a number of Directives concerning the financial sector, notably the Second Banking Directive adopted in December 1989. The Community explained however that, in its final form, the Second Banking Directive reciprocity test is essentially "national treatment" based, and foreign-controlled banking enterprises already operating in a Community country are not subject to the reciprocity test at all.

More generally, recent years have witnessed a growing use of reciprocity in the treatment of foreign investments by host countries, particularly in areas such as banking, insurance and other financial services. While it is true that the principle of reciprocity is often used to promote liberalisation, reciprocity runs counter to the multilateral non-discriminatory approaches and disciplines that form the basis of the open world economic system.

The investment components of bilateral agreements between countries, such as the free trade agreements between Canada and the United States and between Australia and New Zealand, also raise issues concerning the investment climate. Although policies towards enterprises from third countries may remain unchanged, such companies may

19

feel that they are losing out, at least in a relative sense, in that greater liberalisation between the partners to such agreements may not be extended to them.

Another area of concern relates to private sector restrictive practices. The effect of the latter, intended or not, and with more or less tacit approval of governments, is to keep out foreign competition by restraining foreign participation in domestic enterprises, particularly in important areas such as strategic economic and leading technology sectors.

Problems resulting from the imposition by governments of conflicting requirements on multinational enterprises and their negative effects on the investment climate gained in importance in the early 80s. Concerns arise notably when a country's legislation or legal requirements with extraterritorial reach, conflict with legislation or policies in other countries and affect, for instance, the operations of entities of multinational enterprises located in these countries. However, problems in this area have subsided. Countries now understand better the need to combat the avoidance and evasion of domestic laws and regulations, while countries with laws which have an extraterritorial reach have been taking a more careful approach in their application. There has therefore been progress, but efforts are still necessary to consolidate this progress.

In order to achieve the benefits of an open international economy – and these benefits are both clear and substantial – countries must also fully participate in its disciplines. However, the signs of counter-trends evidence a growing concern with the contribution required of and presumed costs to the national economy of openness and liberalisation. It is quite evident, however, that much of the debate questioning the value of international direct investment is based on poor public information and draws sweeping generalisations from particular or clearly limited events, resulting in a rather one-sided perspective, while the benefits to be gained do not seem to figure prominently in these discussions. The remainder of this section seeks to put these concerns under the spotlight.

In the case of issues raised about foreign presence and ownership the following points should be taken into consideration. In the United States, for example, foreign presence is still generally low except in a few sectors but the pace of growth of inward investment has stimulated public interest. Inward investment into the United States comes from a very wide variety of source countries, although Japanese investment may have caught the public eye. In fact, the major single source of international direct investment in the United States continues to be the United Kingdom. In any event, arguments based on trends in the flow of inward investment may give an incomplete if not misleading picture of the full situation. United States inflow data has been subject to quite volatile swings due, inter alia, to changes in the pattern of intra-company transactions. Stock data provide a better indicator of medium and longer term trends and reveal the extent of the United States position abroad and by how much protectionist arguments, therefore, miss the point.

Some of the other concerns with Japanese investment, both inward and outward, also seem not to be supported by the facts. As noted earlier, the relatively low level of international direct investment in Japan is not based on government restrictions, which are limited to a small number of specific sectors (a practice typical of many, even very open, countries). From the point of view of business, the main efforts required to increase international direct investment in Japan are efforts by firms themselves in order to come to terms with doing business in Japan. In the case of "screwdriver operations" issues certainly arise if "sham" foreign investment is a device used to circumvent other restrictions. While there may well have been some clear cases of such screwdriver operations, they are nevertheless very limited in numbers and types in relation to the total amount of international direct investment originating in Japan or other countries in south-east Asia. In fact, many countries welcome assembly facilities, particularly as they have a tendency over time to become more integrated into the host economy; where there is a problem it lies with the circumvention of anti-dumping duties and not with ''screwdriver plants'' per se. Nevertheless, a certain amount of frustration and confusion on the part of investors from these countries can be understood when, in response to criticisms about trade imbalances, companies replace trade by foreign located operations only to find that, depending on the nature of those operations, the same set of criticisms arises on occasion.

The suggested risks that international direct investment may pose to national security seem to have been exaggerated and based on sweeping generalisations from very specific and limited instances. The sectoral or activity pattern of inward investment is very diverse, with no particular penetration in defence and other sensitive areas and no particular concentration by investors from any one country. In any event, all countries quite clearly have the measures at their disposal necessary to protect such interests.

Foreign acquisitions of domestic enterprises have been for some time now a major mode of investing abroad. In the case of the United States for example, restructuring by United States companies and a fall in the dollar exchange rate have provided many candidates for acquisition by other companies, including foreign-based companies. What seems to be forgotten in emotive debates on this subject are the positive effects that acquisitions, including foreign acquisitions, can bring, and the costs that can result if the acquisition does not take place. Restricting acquisitions by foreign companies does not necessarily mean that the gap will be filled by domestic purchasers. In general, acquisitions serve to maintain and generate employment and provide the financial, technical and managerial bases for sounder operation and expansion. The alternative to acquisitions may be stagnation or closure of the firm and a substitution of its output by imports. There is no evidence to suggest that foreign acquisitions in general are suspect in terms of the benefits they bring or their stability and commitment to the domestic economic scene. As indicated earlier, foreign-owned companies generally perform at least as well as their domestic counterparts. Foreign acquisitions also add to savings which are likely to be invested domestically and the associated capital inflow is very welcome in countries with deficit situations. It also often seems to be forgotten that acquisitions represent a major means of investing by United States companies abroad. There is certainly a valid concern about acquisitions, regardless of the nationality of the purchaser, which are based purely on financial strategies or which result in dominant market positions. But these concerns are not related to the nationality of investors and such acquisitions should not be confused with the vast majority of acquisitions which are firmly based on sound business and commercial strategy.

On the basis of the above discussion, protectionist pressures present a danger of backtracking from the significant progress in liberalisation that has been achieved, yet in many instances the reasons for this seem to be based on misplaced fears and economic nationalism rather than on a balanced and comprehensive assessment of the facts. While many governments have been resisting pressures for protectionist moves, there is clearly the potential for an escalation of conflict and retaliatory measures. Such weakening in international disciplines and rules of the game would send a perverse message to non-Member countries, which are being encouraged to liberalise and which have already taken some steps in that direction. This would result in the loss of the very major and widespread advantages that openness has brought.

3. The role of the OECD

The Review period has been one of unprecedented economic and financial integration on a global scale which has given a vital stimulus to the economic development of the OECD area. Moves which now go counter to the liberalisation trend associated with this development are therefore very worrisome, particularly if they persist and develop. Such counter-trends may in fact contribute to uncertainty in an area vital to business, particularly since it is already faced with the actual impact of trade protectionism. These moves may also add to the trends away from multilateralism and a loss of the benefits it has brought.

Action is required, therefore, at the national and international levels to avoid backsliding and to pursue liberalisation. At the national level, administrations should continue to resist protectionist pressures and stimulate a more informed and balanced public debate. At the international level there is a need to relaunch and reinforce international co-operation and disciplines to strengthen and further develop mutual co-operation and understanding between countries and investors.

The OECD has a major role to play in international co-operation and has the means by which these tasks can be pursued. In the light of the above developments it has been strengthening, in some cases quite significantly, these means in the period covered by this Review.

Together with the Codes of Liberalisation of Capital Movements and Current Invisible Operations, the instruments associated with the 1976 OECD Declaration on International Investment and Multinational Enterprises (the Guidelines for Multinational Enterprises, National Treatment, Conflicting Requirements and International Investment Incentives and Disincentives) provide a comprehensive, interlinked and balanced approach to dealing with difficulties which arise in the area of international investment.

The Codes deal with investment by non-resident enterprises including the right of establishment, e.g. limitations on non resident (as opposed to resident) investors affecting the operations of enterprises; and other requirements set at the time of entry or establishment, even if these concern operational requirements. After entry, the treatment accorded to foreign-controlled enterprises operating in Member countries, including new investment by already established foreign-controlled enterprises, is covered by the National Treatment Instrument. On this basis, the Liberalisation Codes and the National Treatment instrument fully cover the investment area.

Since its adoption in 1976, the National Treatment instrument has been strengthened on a number of occasions including the introduction of examinations of Member country exceptions (as of 1984), an understanding not to introduce new exceptions (in 1988) and, in the context of the 1991 Review, the adoption of extensive new commitments to promote the application of the National Treatment instrument in the OECD area. These new commitments reinforce the undertakings of Member countries on standstill and rollback, introduce a requirement of non-discrimination and strengthen further the procedures for the examination of measures constituting exceptions to National Treatment with a view to their progressive elimination (see chapter II). The revised texts of the Declaration and Decisions on International Investment and Multinational Enterprises including the revised National Treatment Instrument, the Guidelines on Multinational Enterprises and Conflicting Requirements are set out in Annexes 1 and 2 to this Report.

The OECD Guidelines for Multinational Enterprises (see chapter III) have an equally important role to play in maintaining an open investment climate. The Guidelines represent Member countries' expectations with respect to the behaviour of multinational enterprises, taking the form of a code of good business conduct for all enterprises. When the Guidelines are followed, and seen to be followed, concerns stemming from the fact that an enterprise is foreign owned are likely to be alleviated. In such a situation, there is then all the more reason for host countries to treat them like domestic enterprises, i.e., accord National Treatment.

In response to problems stemming from conflicting requirements (see chapter IV) the Committee reached an agreement in 1984 on ways and means to deal with such issues. The Committee has agreed to enhance the status of that agreement by integrating the subject of conflicting requirements into the Declaration and by proposing a new Council Decision on this topic. The substance of the 1984 agreement remains unchanged thereby, but the subject is now given the same standing as the other elements of the Declaration. Future efforts of the Committee in respect of conflicting requirements will be geared to consolidating the progress that has since been achieved so far in this area.

The Committee's work in the area of international investment incentives and disincentives is based on the need for international co-operation in this area and the value of greater transparency of government measures. Its recent work (see chapter V) has focused on examining trends in the use of such measures and assessing their impact on international direct investment patterns. The assessment of the effects of disincentives, particularly those likely to have a damaging and wide-reaching effect on the investment climate, such as trade-related investment measures, indicates the benefits to be gained by their abolition and should help reinforce efforts currently underway in the Uruguay Round negotiations to bring such measures under multilateral discipline.

Throughout the Review period, the balance that has characterised the Organisation's approach to international investment questions, including that between the different elements of the 1976 Declaration and Decision on International Investment and Multinational Enterprises, has continued to prevail and will also guide the future work of the Organisation in this area.

Encouraging international direct investment in non-Member countries and contributing to efforts to establish new internationally agreed rules of the game in this area has also proved to be a major challenge. In the Review period, the Committee's work has emphasised efforts to promote the conditions for enhancing international direct investment and its contribution to development (see chapter VI). In addition, and looking particularly to the Dynamic Asian Economies and to central and eastern European countries, growing international interdependence means that more countries will have to share responsibilities, including the observance of clear and equitable rules of the game, if a more integrated global economy is to function well.

Other international fora, too, have been taking initiatives geared to maintaining an open international economy and establishing new rules of the game in the investment area. In the framework of the Uruguay round of GATT negotiations, the trade distorting and restricting effects of trade related investment measures are also being examined. The objective of these negotiations is to bringing such measures under multilateral discipline.

Sufficient progress in this area would have important repercussions on the climate for international direct investment, particularly in respect of the non-Member countries. Under the auspices of the World Bank, the Multilateral Investment Guarantee Agency has now come into operation. Its objective of insuring and protecting international direct investment in the non-Member countries should not only promote such investment but may in the future have positive implications for the treatment of foreign firms in these countries. The United Nations has for some time now been negotiating a code of conduct for transnational corporations, but progress in recent years has not been decisive.

The approaches and efforts in the OECD and elsewhere are complementary. Progress in one area can have important feedback effects on others. OECD efforts and success in investment matters can therefore have wide ranging repercussions. The critical task of these efforts in the period ahead is to reinforce OECD instruments and disciplines, to consolidate the real progress that has been achieved and to contribute to its progressive extension on a global basis.

NOTE

1. The Republic of Korea, Taiwan, Singapore, Hong Kong, Malaysia and Thailand.

Chapter II

NATIONAL TREATMENT

The OECD National Treatment instrument, along with the OECD Codes of Liberalisation, has contributed significantly to the mainly favourable climate for international investment prevailing in the OECD area. Adopted as part of the 1976 Declaration and Decisions on International Investment and Multinational Enterprises, the National Treatment instrument has helped to eliminate discrimination vis-à-vis foreign-controlled enterprises operating in the territories of OECD Member countries. The instrument sets out the principle of National Treatment – that of according treatment to foreign-controlled enterprises operating in Member countries no less favourable than that accorded to domestic enterprises in like situations – and provides the means to promote and extend the application of this principle. Thus, Member countries agreed in 1976 to notify to OECD all government measures that constitute exceptions to National Treatment, to subject these measures to periodic review and to engage in multilateral consultations in respect of any matter relevant to the instrument.

This chapter examines the achievements realised in the area of National Treatment, focusing particularly on the period covered by this Review. It describes briefly, in section 1, the initial work on clarifications and surveying of Member countries' practices in respect of National Treatment, most of which was completed by the time of the 1984 Review. The work on clarifications has had the aim of defining more explicitly the scope of the instrument and how it applies to particular situations. These clarifications provided a basis for a comprehensive survey of Member country measures which in turn led to an improved understanding of the measures in effect, their importance to international investors and their likely impact on the climate for such investment. Efforts subsequently focused on more effective implementation of the instrument, including a more stringent review procedure adopted in 1984 (see section 2) and an understanding on "standstill" in November 1988 pursuant to which Member countries stressed the importance of avoiding the introduction of new measures constituting exceptions to National Treatment. The Committee's discussions have subsequently focused on ways of strengthening the National Treatment instrument. Section 3 describes the progress towards a strengthened instrument and the steps taken to ensure its effective implementation.

The process of extending the application of National Treatment has reinforced the momentum towards liberalisation in the international investment area which has built up since 1976. Each step has consolidated previous achievements while providing a firm basis for the next. At present, however, a number of concerns, already addressed in chapter I, underscore the need to reaffirm international commitments in the investment area and to maintain the discipline that goes hand in hand with such commitments. In the area of National Treatment, Member countries signalled their determination to maintain the momentum so far achieved by recommending the adoption of a Revised Council Decision on National Treatment which reinforces the obligations under the existing Decision relating to the notification and examination of measures contrary to National Treatment. The Committee further agreed that Members should minimise recourse to the instrument's provisions relating to measures motivated by public order and essential security interests so as to achieve a broad application of its liberalisation objectives and a satisfactory overall balance of commitments.

1. Initial work: defining the scope of the instrument and increasing transparency

The first step towards the effective implementation of the newly adopted instrument in 1976 focused on developing a fuller understanding of the scope of the instrument and of how it applied to particular situations. It was also necessary to obtain a better grasp on the situation in Member countries with regard to their application of the principle of National Treatment. For these reasons, the Committee engaged in a process of clarifying the instrument both as regards general aspects and specific categories of measures, and then surveyed National Treatment measures applied in Member countries. The results of that stage of work are reported in depth in *National Treatment for Foreign-Controlled Enterprises,* published in 1985.

Clarifications

In order to provide a basis for increased transparency of relevant government policies and measures and to assist governments in applying the instrument, it was first necessary to clarify its scope of application. Clarifications also serve to determine whether a particular measure is to be considered as an ''exception'' to National Treatment and thus the extent to which the procedures in the National Treatment instrument, and the related procedures established since 1976, apply to the measures in question.

These clarifications addressed, therefore, basic provisions and concepts in the instrument itself as well as how the instrument applies within the various categories into which National Treatment measures have been classified. Clarifications of basic provisions or concepts addressed, for example, the application of National Treatment in areas covered by countries' public order and essential security interests, the meaning of terms such as ''in like situations'', ''operating in their territories'' and ''treatment no less favourable than that accorded to domestic enterprises''. The Committee, together with the Committee on Capital Movements and Invisible Transactions (CMIT), also clarified the relationship between the National Treatment instrument and the Code of Liberalisation of Capital Movements to ensure consistency and completeness in the respective approaches of each instrument. A second group of clarifications addressed the application of National Treatment in the main categories into which measures constituting exceptions to National Treatment have been classified, that is relating to investment by established foreign-controlled enterprises, official aids and subsidies, tax obligations, access to local bank credit and the capital market, and government procurement.

For the most part, the clarifications of the instrument were completed by the time of the 1984 Review. However, the Committee has continued to address issues concerning the application of the instrument in the light of changing circumstances and new developments. A recent example of this concerns the application of National Treatment to the privatisation of enterprises previously under public ownership. The Committee gathered information on areas of government sanctioned monopolies (public, private or mixed) and on areas subject to concession, as well as the nature of the privatisation programmes that have taken place or are underway in many OECD Member countries. It then turned to the implications of these programmes for the application of the instrument. Areas of existing public, private or mixed monopolies are presently recorded under the instrument for the purposes of improving transparency, since foreign-controlled and domestic private enterprises are subject to the same restrictions. The undertaking to apply National Treatment comes into force as and when areas previously under monopoly are opened up. In such cases, access to move into these areas should then be provided on a non-discriminatory basis as between private domestic and foreign-controlled enterprises already established in the country in question. If restrictions prohibit or impede in any way the participation of foreign-controlled enterprises vis-à-vis their domestic counterparts, then these restrictions are to be reported as exceptions to National Treatment. The objective of the instrument in this context is, therefore, to ensure access to formerly closed sectors on an equal basis.

Survey of national treatment measures

With the work on clarifications providing a fuller understanding of the coverage of the instrument, the Committee undertook a comprehensive survey of existing government measures considered to constitute exceptions to National Treatment as well as measures which, while not giving rise to exceptions, the Committee determined should be reported under the instrument for transparency purposes. Transparency is an essential element in efforts to improve the climate for international direct investment. It is also vital to foreign investors who must understand beforehand the treatment they will receive as a result of the laws, regulations and administrative practices of their host countries.

This survey provided Member countries with a more complete and accurate picture of the situation in Member countries with regard to National Treatment – i.e., transparency – and prepared the ground for the subsequent examination of these measures (as discussed in section 2 below). The Committee looked at all types of measures relating to National Treatment in all sectors and covering, for example, the use of prior authorisation or notification requirements associated with investments, ceilings limiting foreign ownership, measures limiting, restricting or prohibiting access or particular modes of entry to sectors or areas of activities such as acquisitions or investments in unrelated areas of activity. Discriminatory or preferential measures often associated with the granting of aids and subsidies, or government purchasing contracts, or differential tax treatment were also covered. The survey addressed measures taken by governments at all relevant levels (including territorial subdivisions) as well as both general and sector specific measures. The motivation for these various measures was also surveyed.

This work resulted in an improved understanding of the measures in effect and of their underlying motivations. On the basis of that survey, a number of conclusions can be drawn as to the broad patterns of measures related to National Treatment found in Member countries. For example, while some measures cover the whole range of business activities (e.g., general authorisation or notification procedures), the vast majority of exceptions to National Treatment are sector-specific and these tend to concentrate on areas such as natural resources, transportation and financial services. In fact, the majority of measures concerns the services sector with only relatively few measures addressed to manufacturing activities. In broad terms, measures are mostly geared to managing the way in which certain areas are opened up to foreign investment and to taking account of specific preoccupations (such as to ensure a degree of protection to specific domestic activities or cultural interests) and not to prevent international direct investment except in specific areas, for example, where a country's public order and essential security interests are prevalent.

The inventory of Member countries' measures relating to National Treatment is kept up-to-date via the examination process (see below) and other ad hoc procedures. The survey and updating process ensures continued transparency. Periodic updating also has the important effect of stimulating countries to take a critical look at the measures they still have and how they compare with those in other countries. This in itself often provides a rationale and an opportunity to remove or relax measures contrary to National Treatment.

2.   The examination of Member country measures related to national treatment

In 1984, the Committee agreed on a strengthened procedure to review the application of the instrument through the periodic examination of measures. In the period covered by this Review, all of the major categories of National Treatment measures have been examined by the Committee. These examinations result in Recommendations, endorsed by the OECD Council, which call upon Member countries to review the totality of their measures constituting exceptions to National Treatment. In certain cases, the Committee may also address specific measures of those countries. These Recommendations propose ways and means by which National Treatment can be extended in the areas covered by the examinations. The effect of these Recommendations, or how they have been implemented by Member countries, cannot yet be fully assessed as, for the most part, sufficient time has not elapsed to permit Member countries to consider and implement them. Nevertheless, there are already signs that the examination procedure is meeting its objectives by the steps to further liberalisation that have been taken by Member countries in the process of individual examinations or subsequent to them.

Examinations

The work on clarification and survey of measures permitted the Committee to focus, after 1984, on developing an approach to strengthening the implementation and extending the application of National Treatment by Member countries. It decided that periodic, in-depth examinations by category and type of measure, for example, investment by established foreign-controlled enterprises, official aids and subsidies, etc., was the most efficient way to proceed. In order to take account of particular areas of concern, the Committee also agreed to look at certain measures on a horizontal basis, cutting across all categories. Measures relating to National Treatment in the services sector, measures applied at the level of territorial subdivisions, and measures taken for public order and essential security interests were selected by the Committee as deserving particular attention in this respect. For example, the examination of measures based on public order and essential security interests was undertaken, inter alia, with a view to ensuring that these considerations are not used as a general escape clause from commitments under the instrument. When it decided to focus on services, the Committee recognised the growth of activities of foreign-controlled enterprises in the services sector as well as the large concentration and relative importance of National Treatment measures maintained therein. It also felt it important to gather information on the extent and application of measures taken at the level of territorial subdivisions of countries in order to increase transparency and ensure that liberalisation efforts also extend to such levels.

Although the examinations so far have been devoted to categories of measures, the Committee has addressed the countries that apply measures in the category under examination. During the examinations, which involve a thorough discussion of the measures, their justification and their continued necessity, the Committee reached conclusions, including conclusions on specific measures of specific countries. The results of examinations are reported to the OECD Council which in turn makes specific Recommendations to Member countries as to the ways in which they should extend the application of National Treatment.

The examination procedure draws particular attention to measures which, by their severity, coverage or reach are likely to have the most significant impact on the activities of foreign-controlled enterprises, measures of specific concern, as well as measures taken by only a few countries in areas where other countries do not appear to have any need to impose similar restrictions affecting National Treatment.

Effects of exceptions to national treatment

The Committee's discussion of the impact of exceptions to National Treatment serves two main purposes. First, it is one of the elements taken into account by the Committee in proposing Recommendations and in focusing, within these, on particular measures. Secondly, it provides indications of the costs to enterprises and national economies that can arise from restrictions, thereby emphasising the benefits to be gained from an extension of National Treatment.

The impact of a given exception to National Treatment depends on various factors including, for example the severity or degree of restrictiveness of the measure, the number and importance of firms and sectors affected and the number of countries applying the measure in question. Also relevant is the extent to which discretionary measures are applied. A number of countries have reported discretionary powers which have never or only very exceptionally been used. Clearly, the non-application of such measures is seen as a positive feature from the perspective of the instrument, but the mere existence of such measures does, nevertheless, contain the potential for discriminatory application, and as such they are reported as exceptions.

On the basis of the work of the Committee, as well as contributions by BIAC (Business and Industry Advisory Committee to OECD) and analysis of other bodies in the OECD in respect of particular sectors, some general remarks can be made. Measures of the type covered in the category ''investment by established foreign-controlled enterprises'', such as outright prohibitions, strict authorisation procedures, restrictions on acquisitions or foreign ownership levels, etc. are generally found to be the most onerous to business. Such measures may result in significant modification if not outright abandonment of investments and may well discourage others from considering particular investments. For those investments which nevertheless go ahead, the impact of restrictions may be to hinder the ability of thefirm to compete on an equal footing with domestic counterparts. Measures of the types listed above do seem, from the point of view of business, more onerous than exceptions to National Treatment in areas such as government procurement or official aids and subsidies. Discrimination in these latter areas may, nevertheless, place foreign-controlled enterprises at important cost disadvantages which may affect their longer term health and viability. While discriminatory treatment in areas such as tax obligations or access to finance and the local capital market may pose difficulties for individual firms, restrictions in such areas are of generally lesser concern to business, not least because there are relatively few discriminatory practices in these areas. Aside from losses or costs to foreign enterprises themselves as a result of discriminatory measures, it should not be forgotten that there are also costs to the host economy in general, including those resulting from lost technology, jobs, competition and management skills.

Recommendations

The Recommendations proposed by the Committee and adopted by the OECD Council on the basis of the completed examinations include general Recommendations urging, for example, Member countries to examine the totality of their measures related to National Treatment and to consider their possible removal or relaxation. Member countries are also invited to consider alternative ways and means of addressing particular concerns or pursuing particular objectives which would be more consistent with the principle of National Treatment. As part of these general Recommendations, Member countries are urged to limit the application of their measures so as not to exceed the field of concern underlying the measure.

In addition, the Committee has felt it important to highlight specific measures by formulating Recommendations addressed to particular measures of countries. For example, trans-sectoral exceptions restricting investment by foreign-controlled enterprises (such as authorisation/notification requirements, review of acquisitions, prohibitions or limitations on foreign ownership) have been singled out and the countries which cannot remove such measures are urged to narrow their scope by making them more specific. The importance attached to the liberalisation of international services operations led to specific Recommendations in the context of the examination of measures in the services sector, proposing, inter alia, that countries give particular attention to ensuring that moves towards privatisation of service sector activities result in increasing the opportunities for both domestic and foreign-controlled enterprises alike to invest in these activities. Similarly, concerns with measures prohibiting or restricting acquisitions were addressed in the examination of measures in the "investment by established foreign-controlled enterprises" category. In other areas, and given the Committee's finding that discriminatory measures may have wider reverberations than just the immediate restriction on a particular activity, countries maintaining the measures in question which can distort or jeopardise the competitive position of foreign-controlled enterprises have been recommended to remove, relax, or limit the scope of application of these measures. Throughout these Recommendations, Member countries have been invited, wherever relevant, to endeavour to ensure that the Recommendations also extend to measures taken by the territorial subdivisions of countries.

Results of examinations and patterns of liberalisation

The objective of the examinations described above is to encourage Member countries to extend the application of National Treatment. The process of highlighting certain of their measures and the detailed discussion on the assessment of effects and comparison with other countries' measures, brings pressure on countries to remove or relax their exceptions to National Treatment.

While the Committee has now completed the first round of examinations of the major categories of measures, it is still too early to assess fully the effect given to the Recommendations concerning the measures examined. It is evident, nonetheless, that the examination procedure itself has already contributed to the removal or relaxation of restrictions.

Investment policies in OECD Member countries have become strikingly more open with regulations and practices pertaining to foreign-controlled enterprises being increasingly aligned with the principle of National Treatment. In general, this progress can be seen as part of the overall movement away from impediments, obstacles and restrictions to foreign direct investment as well as in moves to deregulation and privatisation. Examples of the extension of National Treatment include the removal or raising of foreign ownership ceilings, the abandonment of measures limiting or prohibiting certain activities of foreign-controlled enterprises, the adoption of non-discriminatory approaches in areas such as government procurement and the removal or relaxation of measures previously requiring authorisation or prior notification. Indeed, in respect of the latter types of measures, there are numerous examples of the relaxation and simplification of procedures and efforts to increase their flexibility and fairness. Greater liberalisation is found throughout a broad range of activities such as oil and gas and other primary industries, manufacturing and service sector activities such as financial services, tourism and telecommunications.

Restrictions of various kinds have thus tended to decrease very significantly in the OECD area in the last decade. Of course, OECD countries have not started this liberalisation process from the same degree of restrictiveness, so that differences still remain with respect to the degree of severity of the restrictions they retain. Some countries, for example, maintain their long-standing tradition of openness to foreign investors, sometimes despite internal pressures to be more restrictive which governments, so far, have been able to withstand. Other countries, in the past much more restrictive, have certainly become more liberal; some of these have now removed all but a few sector specific restrictions; in others, however, regulations remain complex and restrictive and recent moves to liberalisation are still incomplete.

Overall, the trend towards reduction of restrictions and simplification of practices is significant. Nevertheless, there remain restrictions and impediments which still give cause for concern. Even in the most liberal countries, for example, foreign investors may still encounter remaining sectoral restrictions. It is not uncommon to find such restrictions in natural resources and energy as well as in the services sectors, particularly in areas such as banking, insurance, transportation and the media.

While some countries have removed measures based on reciprocity and others have shown restraint in avoiding them, reciprocity remains a feature of concern in policies towards foreign investment in certain fields, notably banking and insurance. It is true that extreme forms of reciprocity (e.g. retroactive measures) have been avoided, nevertheless the Committee stands by its earlier clarification that reciprocity measures ultimately conflict with multilateral approaches to liberalisation. Similarly, the Committee is concerned that agreements resulting from bilateral or regional arrangements, extend the application of National Treatment on a non-discriminatory and OECD-wide basis. Finally, the Committee is maintaining its attention on privatisation programmes in Member countries with a view to ensuring that the activities concerned are opened up to all private investors on a non-discriminatory basis.

The Committee has given much consideration in recent years to consolidating the progress achieved. It has therefore closely followed the developments, described in Chapter I, that are giving rise to frictions between Member countries and that could put this progress in jeopardy. These unfavourable developments underline the need for continued vigilance concerning the application of National Treatment. Protectionism in other areas, particularly in the field of trade, could also have detrimental effects in the investment area. It is in this context that the Committee undertook to strengthen the National Treatment instrument.

3. Strengthening national treatment commitments

Recognising the importance of reinforcing the commitments undertaken in 1976, the OECD Ministers mandated the CIME in May 1988 to examine ways and means of further strengthening the National Treatment instrument. The Committee responded quickly with the adoption, in November 1988, of an understanding on a standstill with respect to new measures or practices constituting exceptions to National Treatment[1]. This standstill has been respected except for one known breach[2].

At the OECD Ministerial Council meeting on 4-5 June, 1991 Ministers noted the progress towards a strengthening of the National Treatment instrument inspired by the principles of standstill, non-discrimination, transparency and rollback and agreed to reinforce the procedures for implementing the existing substantive commitments through notification, examination and a multilateral framework for dealing with conflicts that may arise. They also expressed their determination to further reinforce and broaden the scope of international discipline in the area of foreign direct investment.

The Council agreed on the need to seek further liberalisation through continued efforts to improve the instrument and encouraged closer co-operation between the Committee on International Investment and Multinational Enterprises and the Committee on Capital Movements and Invisible Transactions to pursue the liberalisation of foreign direct investment policies, including entry and establishment and the treatment of established foreign-controlled enterprises. The Council also invited the Secretary-General to prepare a study to explore the advantages and feasibility of a broader investment instrument. This study could take into account inter alia the evolution in investment flows and investment instruments and should draw as appropriate, on relevant provisions of the National Treatment instrument and the Codes of Liberalisation. The study could also take into account other principles embodied in Member countries' bilateral investment treaties and examine the possibility of establishing strengthened dispute settlement procedures.

As a first step, strengthened procedures for implementing the National Treatment commitments have since been put in place by amending the Council Decision on National Treatment. Following adoption of these new procedures, the National Treatment instrument consists of:

- The existing Section on National Treatment of the 1976 Declaration on International Investment and Multinational Enterprises (hereafter the "Declaration") which sets out Member countries' political commitments concerning National Treatment; and
- The Third Revised Decision on National Treatment as amended in 1991 (hereafter the "Decision") which sets out the legally binding obligations concerning notification and examination of exceptions, as well as procedures for dispute settlement.

The European Economic Community intends to participate as a Member in the section on National Treatment of the Declaration and in the Revised Decision.

The Declaration contains the general undertaking that Member countries will accord National Treatment to foreign-controlled enterprises operating in their territories. Member countries with territorial subdivisions with non-subordinated powers endeavour to ensure that their territorial subdivisions apply National Treatment. The Revised Decision, however, applies to all Members regarding measures taken at the level of territorial subdivisions as well as by the central government. The full text of the 1976 Declaration and the Third Revised Decision on National Treatment are reproduced in Annexes 1 and 2.

Strengthened procedures for promoting national treatment

Enhancing the transparency of Members' measures relating to National Treatment is assured by the obligations contained in the Revised Decision to notify all such measures to the OECD. Moreover, all exceptions to National Treatment will be listed in an Annex to the Decision. Other measures with a bearing on National Treatment (e.g., those taken for reasons of public order and essential security interests) are notified for transparency purposes. The notification procedures and the listing of exceptions promote a comprehensive investigation by Members of their measures which may have a bearing on the instrument.

Procedures have been incorporated in the Revised Decision which permit reference to the Organisation for all matters concerning the Declaration and Revised Decision on National Treatment. The Committee will serve as the forum for consultations in such cases and will then report to the Council on the results, including proposals it may wish to make to the Member countries concerned.

A strengthened examination procedure is a key element in promoting progressive liberalisation. Whereas examinations have so far been conducted on the basis of categories of measures contrary to National Treatment, the strengthened instrument provides that examinations be carried out on a country-by-country basis, while allowing for other approaches as necessary. The country-by-country examination procedure will provide a stronger thrust towards liberalisation as greater pressure concentrates, at the time of the examination, on a single country. A follow-up will normally take place within a year after a country has been examined to determine the effect given to the recommendations made at the time of the examination.

Clarifying the scope of the instrument

The Committee paid particular attention to measures justified by public order and essential security interests. It reaffirmed that the provisions of the instrument which permit these measures to be classified as transparency items rather than exceptions should not be used as a general escape clause from countries' commitments by shielding measures in fact taken for economic, cultural or other reasons. Indeed, the Committee considered that excessive recourse to these provisions might weaken the application of the instrument and raise questions about the overall balance of commitments by Member countries. The Committee concluded that Member countries should reduce to a bare minimum the number of measures classified as being motivated by public order or essential security interests, and that where motivations are mixed (e.g. partly commercial and partly national security), the measures concerned should be covered by exceptions rather than merely recorded for transparency purposes.

The Committee developed clarifications on the National Treatment instrument's relation to the Codes of Liberalisation in order to establish a clear operational dividing line between the respective fields of application of these instruments. To avoid a technical overlap with the Codes' coverage of non-resident investment, the Committee agreed to exclude, for National Treatment purposes, the investment activities of "direct" branches, (i.e. branches whose parent company is a non-resident) since these branches could not be considered legally capable of direct investment operations on their own account. This exclusion applies only to measures in the investment by established foreign controlled enterprises category, while measures in all other categories affecting direct branches continue to be covered by the National Treatment Instrument, measures affecting invest- ment by direct branches are covered by the Code of Liberalisation of Capital Movements. Measures affecting investment by indirect branches (i.e. branches whose parent company is an established subsidiary of a non-resident) continue to be covered by the National Treatment instrument in the same way that all operations of subsidiaries are covered.

The Committee also looked at the question of discriminatory membership conditions applied by stock exchanges, associations or regulatory bodies, and agreed that such measures or practices should be covered by the instrument where discrimination is based on nationality. This applies to restrictive conditions concerning membership irrespective of whether there is full, partial or no governmental involvement in the setting of such conditions. This approach parallels the new obligations adopted by Member countries under the Revised Codes of Liberalisation[3].

Improved transparency of national treatment measures

The Committee has undertaken an exhaustive review of the measures maintained by Members which may be contrary to the principle of National Treatment. This work has resulted in a better understanding of the nature and scope of these measures. It has also enabled the Committee to make a clear distinction between measures considered excep- tions to National Treatment and subject to the full disciplines of the instrument, and those reported only for transparency purposes, such as measures concerning public/private and mixed monopolies and areas of concession, and corporate organisation measures (requirements providing for a majority participation of nationals of the host country in the management and/or the board of directors of an enterprise). In some cases, it was possible to determine that the measures concerned did not need to be reported at all since no discrimination was involved on the basis of nationality[4].

This exercise also permitted the Committee to gather more information on measures maintained at the level of territorial subdivisions, thereby increasing transparency and providing a basis for surveillance of measures at all levels. In so doing, Member countries were better able to determine whether a satisfactory balance of commitments had been achieved under the instrument and where the efforts of the Committee should concentrate so as to encourage continued liberalisation of policies towards foreign direct investment.

The National Treatment instrument will be reviewed by the Committee within three years. This review will provide an opportunity to assess the progress achieved by all members in applying National Treatment. The Committee will report to the Council on the results of this review and will make proposals for strengthening the commitments on National Treatment at all levels.

The Committee's work on a strengthened National Treatment instrument has provided a more solid basis for implementing Members' commitments to National Treatment. This results both from the adoption of stronger procedures in the Revised Council Decision and a better understanding of the nature of the measures in place. In this process, Members reviewed their measures to determine whether they were in conformity with the principles of a strengthened instrument. In so doing, they have confirmed their commitment to a multilateral framework for promoting the liberalisation of foreign direct investment policies.

NOTES AND REFERENCES

1. The understanding reached by the Committee on International Investment and Multinational Enterprises on a standstill on National Treatment Measures in November 1988 was as follows: "In the context of its continued discussion of extending the application of National Treatment, the Committee noted that Ministers had also called for the avoidance of back-sliding by Member countries (Ministerial Council communiqué of 19th May 1988). In order to comply with the intention expressed by Ministers in this regard, the Committee stressed that it is particularly important, in the period leading up to the completion of the 1990 Review of the OECD 1976 Declaration and Decisions on International Investment and Multinational Enterprises and to the adoption of a possible new and strengthened National Treatment instrument, that Member countries avoid the introduction of new measures or practices which constitute exceptions to the present National Treatment instrument. The Committee further agreed that it would pay particular attention to this question in its regular follow-up of changes in practices and policies in Member countries."

2. The United States notified the CIME in February 1991 of a new exception in the category of official aids and subsidies (reciprocity conditions for participation in the Advanced Technology Programme).

3. See *Liberalisation of Capital Movements and Financial Services in the OECD Area*, OECD 1990.

4. This is the case, for example, for measures determined to be "equivalent treatment" as defined in the Committee's Report on the National Treatment instrument, and for measures based on residency, as opposed to nationality, requirements.

Chapter III

THE GUIDELINES FOR MULTINATIONAL ENTERPRISES

The Guidelines for Multinational Enterprises are recommendations jointly addressed by the OECD governments to multinational enterprises operating in their territories. They represent the collective expectations of these governments concerning the behaviour and activities of multinational enterprises. Observance of the Guidelines is voluntary and not legally enforceable. Their objective is to provide guidance to multinational enterprises by setting standards addressed to these enterprises. In particular, they should help ensure that their operations are in harmony with the national policies of the countries where they operate and to strengthen the basis of mutual confidence between enterprises and governments.

The Guidelines are a key component of the OECD approach to increasing international co-operation and mutual understanding in the field of international direct investment and to improving the economic climate for that investment. They are fully supported by business and labour, as represented in the OECD by the Business and Industry Advisory Committee (BIAC) and the Trade Union Advisory Committee (TUAC), as well as national business organisations and form part of a balanced framework of interrelated instruments under the 1976 Declaration and Decision on International Investment and Multinational Enterprises. Inter-relations with other elements of this package, such as National Treatment and conflicting requirements have already been illustrated in chapter I and show the mutually reinforcing character of these instruments.

The recommendations of the Guidelines cover the full range of business activities and operations. Their objective is to encourage the positive contributions which multinational enterprises can make to economic and social progress and to minimise and resolve the difficulties to which their various operations may give rise. They are firmly based on the principle of non-discrimination and are therefore not aimed at introducing differences of treatment between multinational and domestic enterprises; wherever relevant, they reflect good practice for all, such that both groups of enterprises are subject to the same expectations in respect of their conduct.

The work of the Committee and its Working Group on the Guidelines in this field since 1976 has been guided by the desire to maintain the stability of the Guidelines, which is an important feature in assuring their acceptance and implementation by enterprises, the balance with respect to the other components of the 1976 Declaration and sufficient flexibility in the instrument to allow it to meet new developments and concerns.

The Committee has devoted important efforts to ensure the continuing relevance of the Guidelines, and to follow their implementation. This work has included surveys of experience with the Guidelines and their associated procedures in Member countries and studies of relevant developments with a view to ensuring that these are fully covered by the Guidelines. The Committee has continued to clarify, as the need arises, the coverage and intentions of the Guidelines with respect to specific situations. It has decided to introduce a new chapter in the Guidelines on the protection of the environment in response to the significant concerns that have developed in this area. The Committee also gives high priority to promoting awareness and implementation of the Guidelines by enterprises. Indeed, it has singled this out as one of the key areas where efforts should be further developed if the Guidelines are to continue to play an important role in promoting a good climate for international direct investment.

Looking back to 1976, the Guidelines can be seen as part of the Organisation's response to concerns that had arisen in the field of international investment and multinational enterprises. In the following years, the Guidelines have made a significant contribution to the evolution in attitudes and experience that has been achieved. By providing a means whereby multinational enterprises can demonstrate that they are good corporate citizens, the Guidelines have played a valuable role in improving the level of confidence in this area and the climate for international investment. The Guidelines have proved to be a realistic, balanced and flexible framework within which multinational enterprises can operate, while the work of the Committee on the Guidelines has helped to demystify the multinational phenomenon and, in so doing, alleviated or dissipated earlier fears or concerns.

When introduced in 1976, the Guidelines represented a very innovative instrument, being the first internationally agreed framework for co-operation in the field of international direct investment and multinational enterprises, which was also accepted and supported by business and labour. Since then, the Guidelines have been used to varying extents as a reference for other international instruments such as the International Labour Office's Tripartite Declaration of Principles concerning Multinational Enterprises and Social Policy, the set of Mutually Agreed Equitable Principles and Rules for the Control of Restrictive Business Practices agreed in the United Nations and the draft United Nations Code of Conduct for Transnational Corporations.

The Guidelines are therefore important to governments as an integral part of their approach to dealing with issues linked to international investment and multinational enterprises. They also provide a common framework, agreed to by business and labour within which discussion and consultation on matters covered by the Guidelines can be held.

A decade and a half later, the Guidelines have stood the test of time remarkably well, spanning a period of unsettled global economic conditions followed by strong economic recovery, as well as major changes in the patterns and forms of international direct investment and the ways in which multinational enterprises organise their operations. The Guidelines' strength can be traced to their stability and balance over time which has provided a predictable environment in which to operate. This stability does not mean inflexibility. As this chapter shows, the Organisation is ready to make modifications to the Guidelines when it determines that such a step is necessary to deal with new situations or growing concerns.

Issues related to the activities of multinational enterprises, of course, do continue to arise. The key point is that when they do, the Guidelines provide a well-established mechanism which has demonstrated its usefulness in dealing with such questions. The

Guidelines have contributed significantly to the more positive attitudes and approaches to multinational enterprises and the development of a more open climate for international direct investment.

This chapter looks at the Guidelines in relation to the development of international co-operation in the field of international investment and multinational enterprises. It traces, in Section 1, how attitudes towards multinational enterprises have changed since the introduction of the Guidelines in 1976 and the role of the Guidelines in this evolution. Section 2 reports on the main elements of the work on the Guidelines by the Committee since the last Review in 1984. Section 3 indicates the tasks in the years ahead and the important contribution the Guidelines can make in maintaining an open investment climate.

1. Changing attitudes to multinational enterprises and the role of the Guidelines

When the Guidelines were introduced in 1976, the general economic situation, as well as the environment for international direct investment and multinational enterprises, was very different from that prevailing today. At that time, multinational enterprises were often the focus of widespread and critical attention in many countries. Considered by some to be excessively large and powerful and in some respects beyond the authority of the individual sovereign state, they were alleged in some cases to use this power disruptively. Typical concerns included the abuse of dominant market positions, a lack of commitment to the host economy or insufficient integration in the domestic business environment. Questions were raised about the stability of their operations and decisions taken on the basis of global corporate strategies not necessarily linked to the local situation. In response to concerns that the benefits of international direct investment were skewed in favour of the multinational enterprise, many countries, as noted in chapter I, placed controls or restrictions on international direct investment, in some instances to exclude or limit such investment; in others in an attempt to ensure the contributions of international direct investment to the host economy. To varying degrees, a certain number of OECD countries held this generalised view of multinational enterprises, but it was particularly pronounced in the developing countries.

Since then perceptions of and attitudes towards multinational enterprises have evolved considerably, not least in OECD countries. While many factors are responsible for this development, much of it can be linked to trends in international direct investment and experience with and the performance of multinational enterprises. The Guidelines have contributed by providing a common frame of reference and by assisting multinational enterprises to ensure that their operations and activities are compatible with the expectations of host countries.

As discussed in chapter I, changes in international direct investment patterns have resulted in a more liberal approach to such investment by OECD countries. International direct investment has become more ubiquitous and at the same time more diverse. A growing number of countries play an active role as both home and host countries. Greater diversity in international direct investment has also diffused many previous concerns. For example, no one single country dominates international direct investment flows and the greater sectoral spread has reduced fears that international direct investment was concentrated in a few key, sensitive areas. Moreover, the operations of multinational enterprises cover a growing variety of forms including joint ventures, sub-contracting and other arrangements between separate companies which have brought new and valued relationships with local investors and governments.

Experience with the performance of multinational enterprises over the intervening years, covering both difficult as well as periods of strong recovery and growth, has also been important. By and large, multinational enterprises have met the challenge of reacting quickly and flexibly to rapid changes in technologies, market conditions and the business environment. The Committee's study of *Structural Adjustment and Multinational Enterprises,* published in 1985, has shown, for example, that multinational enterprises have made a positive contribution to adjustment and growth as they have often been able to adjust more flexibly, sometimes in anticipation of pressures, due to their managerial, financial and technical position. Their employment performance has been generally at least equal, and in some cases superior, to that of domestic enterprises. Also, on the basis of available evidence, it appears that multinational enterprises are no more likely to resort to the closure or transfer of entities than are their domestic counterparts. Multinationals have also been aware of and concerned with their image and have taken various steps designed to improve it or to develop a more balanced public awareness of their activities. Enterprises have displayed over time a greater awareness of the importance of public policy issues and public perception of the role of multinational enterprises, where growing interest or concern in particular fields has been paralleled by private sector actions, for example in the environmental area where the International Chamber of Commerce has adopted environmental guidelines for world industry.

Through the efforts of the Committee, Member countries, BIAC and TUAC, the Guidelines have been closely associated with these changing perceptions and, more generally, with the progress towards liberalisation described in chapter I. The remainder of this section looks at these efforts in the area of promotion, implementation and follow-up, including the general procedure followed by the Guidelines.

Member countries have reported that the level of observance of the Guidelines appears to be generally high. The Guidelines are compatible with domestic laws, regulations and policies which enterprises are required to follow. Also they have been endorsed by major business organisations. These factors, together with the balance and stability that characterises the Guidelines have contributed to their acceptance and implementation. During discussions in the Committee it has been suggested that further efforts would be useful in promoting the contribution that the Guidelines may make in providing a framework for reference in discussions between management and labour in areas such as collective bargaining.

Of course, in some instances, issues or difficulties still arise from the activities of individual multinational enterprises. Multinational, like domestic enterprises, still close activities or make other changes in their operations which may pose difficulties for labour or host governments. For example, concerns still arise when key decisions affecting the foreign located subsidiary are taken elsewhere, when there are difficulties in labour having access to those responsible for decision making, when information necessary for collective bargaining is lacking or when the parent company places restrictions or limits on certain of the activities of the foreign located subsidiary. These and other types of issues raised by TUAC and by some Member countries which have been addressed by the Committee in the period since the last Review are reported below in Section 2.

Seeking to keep abreast of recent trends and developments in the field of international investment and multinational enterprises and to ensure that the Guidelines maintain their relevance over time the Committee periodically undertakes analytical studies. Mention can be made, for example, of the report published in 1987 on *Recent Trends in International Direct Investment* and the study on *Structural Adjustment and Multinational Enterprises* published in 1985, the latter of which was conducted within the framework of the 1984 Review. In the context of the present Review, the Committee published a study on the *Structure and Organisation of Multinational Enterprises* in 1987, the results of which are reported in Section 2 below.

That issues still arise from the activities of multinational enterprises demonstrates the importance of continuing to promote knowledge and implementation of the Guidelines. This is an area to which the Committee attaches high importance. Together with Member countries, BIAC and TUAC, the Committee has devoted important efforts to this area, including for example, publication and translation of texts related to the Guidelines, circulars and letters of support from BIAC and business organisations to enterprises, articles in the publications and brochures of government and business and labour organisations, and workshops and training programmes. The publication by the OECD in 1986 of *The OECD Guidelines for Multinational Enterprises,* which brings together all of the work of the Committee on the Guidelines since 1976, is considered by the Committee to be one of its major accomplishments in this area in the Review period. It is also intended that publication of the present Review report will further contribute to this objective.

The Committee has agreed that promotional efforts should be maintained in the period ahead. One reason for this is that the ''population'' to which the Guidelines are addressed, as noted earlier, has been changing, as international direct investment has grown and its patterns have become much more diversified, and as new multinational enterprises are created. BIAC has stated that it will increase its efforts to promote and support the Guidelines by encouraging enterprises to spread knowledge of them throughout their organisations, via such means as seminars, training courses and internal company communications.

The National Contact Points, which have been set up by all Member countries to deal with matters related to the Guidelines at the local level, have an important role to play in the promotion of the Guidelines and their follow-up. National Contact Points provide facilities for handling enquiries and for discussion with the parties concerned on matters relating to the Guidelines. In some cases, National Contact Points have also played an important role in bringing issues to the attention of the Committee. While the institutional patterns and variety of functions conducted by the National Contact Points vary from country to country, common functions involve the dissemination, promotion and, to the extent necessary, explanation of the Guidelines, the provision of a forum for discussion, particularly with business and trade unions, on problems which may arise in relation to the Guidelines, and engaging in direct contacts with other National Contact Points where necessary. In providing such facilities, the National Contact Points can usefully contribute, within the framework of national laws and practices, to the solution of problems related to the Guidelines that may arise.

In the context of this Review, the Committee has examined the role and functioning of the National Contact Points. Member countries expressed satisfaction with the manner in which they have carried out their responsibilities in general, including promotional activities of the Guidelines, the handling of enquiries and facilitating the resolution of issues at the national level. The Committee considered that National Contact Points can make more significant contributions to the understanding and acceptance of the Guidelines. In particular, when issues arise and when they are signalled by one National Contact Point to another, the National Contact Points should ensure that the enterprises concerned are aware of the Guidelines, as well as clarifications issued by the Committee. National Contact Points can also ensure that enterprises are fully informed of the importance that governments attach to the Guidelines.

2. Discussions and conclusions on issues relating to the Guidelines

An important objective of the Committee's work is that enterprises understand clearly the expectations of governments as expressed in the Guidelines with regard to the range of activities and operations they cover. It is also necessary that the Guidelines address new concerns and developments. An important element of the Committee's work is, therefore, to clarify the provisions of the Guidelines or to propose to the Council amendments to the text of the Guidelines where necessary. This section reports the work undertaken by the CIME in respect of these tasks over the period since the 1984 Review. Work up to that time has been brought together in the 1986 Guidelines publication referred to above.

Of course, not all discussion of the intentions of the Guidelines in respect of specific situations or their scope and coverage in particular fields needs to result in new clarifications. The Guidelines, after all, have achieved a certain maturity which is associated with a considerable background to the interpretation of their scope and intentions throughout the full range of business activities and operations. Together with this, the Committee's approach of focusing on issues related to the Guidelines and not on whether specific actions of individual enterprises are in conformity with the expectations set out in the Guidelines, has meant that over time many of the key questions on their scope and application have already been clarified. Nevertheless, discussion on the expectations of the Guidelines in respect of specific events permits fruitful exchanges of views between Member countries, BIAC and TUAC and helps to consolidate established understandings and approaches.

Clarifications are issued by the Committee in response to questions raised, explaining in more detail the meaning of existing provisions in order to assist the parties concerned when using the Guidelines. They should not be considered as modifying the Guidelines but they do carry the weight of a joint understanding reached by OECD Member countries on the scope and meaning of the Guidelines. Amendments to the text of the Guidelines have been relatively rare and infrequent – not only do the Guidelines present a comprehensive set of recommendations covering the full range of business operations and activities, but the Committee firmly believes that their stability has been a crucial factor in their continued acceptance by enterprises and has made a strong contribution to confidence in their effectiveness. The overall approach of the Committee, therefore, has been to maintain the stability of the Guidelines while ensuring sufficient flexibility to meet new situations or growing concerns.

In the context of the present Review the Committee has provided a number of clarifications with respect to issues raised and also has agreed to introduce a new chapter of the Guidelines on the topic of environmental protection. The details of this new chapter, as well as clarifications and discussions of other issues raised in respect of the Guidelines, are presented below.

Employee representation and reasonable notice

Issues related to the right of employees to be represented by trade unions or other bona fide organisation of employees and to the provision of reasonable notice to representatives of employees when enterprises are considering changes in their operations which would have major effects on the livelihood of employees have been discussed by the Committee on a number of occasions. Such issues are addressed, in particular, by paragraphs 1 and 6, respectively, of the Employment and Industrial Relations Guidelines.

In the period covered by the present Review, complaints concerning anti-union activities in certain multinational enterprises have been brought to the attention of the Committee on a number of occasions. It thus appears that problems in this area continue to arise whereby not only the right of employees to be represented may not be respected but also that in specific instances, active efforts may have been undertaken to discourage organising activities of employees. The Committee regrets that such situations continue to exist or arise and takes the present opportunity to stress again the provisions of the Guidelines as these apply to the question of employee representation. The Committee has therefore reaffirmed the view already expressed in both the 1979 and 1984 Review Reports that the thrust of the Guidelines in this area is towards management adopting a positive approach towards the activities of trade unions and an open attitude towards organisational activities of workers in the framework of national rules and practices.

The Committee has also clarified two particular issues linking the notions of employee representation and the provision of notice to employees which were brought to its attention following events in a Member country. The first of these issues concerns the interpretation of the term ''representatives of employees'' in the absence of recognised trade unions or any other existing form of collective representation in an enterprise.

In responding to the questions raised on the notion of employee representation in the context of paragraph 6 of the Employment and Industrial Relations Guidelines, the Committee considered it important to recall that paragraph 6 reflects agreement among Member countries' governments that when enterprises consider changes in their operations which would have major effects upon the likelihood of their employees, it is very important that representatives of their employees should be provided with reasonable notice of such changes, and that the enterprise co-operates so as to mitigate, to the maximum extent practicable, adverse effects.

The Committee recalls that the Guidelines provide that enterprises should, within the framework of national law, regulations and prevailing labour relations practices, ''respect the right of their employees to be represented by trade unions and other bona fide organisations of employees.'' Nevertheless, enterprises may on occasion be faced with a situation where their employees are not represented. While paragraph 6 of the Employment and Industrial Relations Guidelines addresses situations where employees are represented, the Committee has clarified that where this is not the case, enterprises should take all practical steps towards addressing the objectives underlying paragraph 6 of the Employment and Industrial Relations chapter within the framework of national laws, regulations and prevailing labour relations practices.

The second question addressed in the same context was that of whether, in interpreting the term ''reasonable notice of changes in operations'', account should be taken of

43

the view of an enterprise that the sensitivity of its business decision or the sensitivity of the jobs of individuals should materially affect the provision of "reasonable notice".

Here, the Committee recalled that the Guidelines are not aimed at introducing rigid rules that would make the tasks of management more difficult. The Committee also considered that there may be circumstances in which the sensitivity of business decisions and/or of particular jobs, in terms of possible serious damage to the enterprises concerned, is such that it would render it difficult for them, when considering changes in their activities which would have major effects on the livelihood of their employees, to give their representatives early notice of such changes. However, it is the view of the Committee that such circumstances would be exceptional. In particular, there is no business sector or business activity where it could be considered that such circumstances would usually prevail.

The Committee also considered it useful to recall that paragraph 6 of the Employment and Industrial Relations Guidelines implies that enterprises should, in the relevant circumstances, be in any case in a position to co-operate with employee representatives and appropriate governmental authorities so as to mitigate to the maximum extent practicable the adverse effects of the changes in their operations. It is implied that the notice of changes in their operations should be given and the implementation of these changes should be done in such a way that the meaningful co-operation indicated in the Guidelines can take place.

In the light of the very specific nature of the two categories of questions addressed above, the Committee has emphasised that the clarifications it has given are not aimed at providing a full definition or clarification of the terms "representatives of employees" and "reasonable notice" for the purposes of the Guidelines. In fact, the Committee's discussions, in line with the questions raised, only touched on certain aspects of the understanding of these terms and their implications for the Guidelines.

Information provision to the general public

The provision of information by multinational enterprises on their structure and activities is fundamental to the objectives the Guidelines seek to achieve. The Committee's discussions of information provision over the Review period have focused on two main areas of the Guidelines, the provision of information to the general public (addressed in the chapter on the Disclosure of Information), which is discussed in this section and the provision of information to employees (covered by the chapter on Employment and Industrial Relations) which is discussed in the next.

The purpose of the chapter of the Guidelines on Disclosure of Information is to give greater transparency to the activities multinational enterprises through the publication of a sufficient body of information to improve public understanding. In so doing, concerns which arise from the complexity of multinational enterprises and the difficulties in clearly perceiving their diverse structures, operations and policies can be alleviated. The significance of this task has been clearly shown in the discussion of chapter I, where it has been suggested that improved public information and understanding in the area of international direct investment and multinational enterprises could make a significant contribution to a favourable investment climate.

Experience has shown that a number of accounting terms and disclosure items in the chapter on Disclosure of Information required further explanation to assist enterprises in complying with them. In 1983, a first set of clarifications was published. As a result of the work carried out since the 1984 Review Report, the Committee has issued a number of new clarifications on the structure of the enterprise and on consolidation policies. Moreover, specific disclosure and accounting issues arise with respect to the Guidelines in the field of financial services. For this reason, the Committee issued specific clarifications for disclosure by banks and insurance companies and for operating results by banks. Finally, the reports adopted by the Committee on income tax accounting and foreign currency translation have led to a revision of earlier clarifications.

The Working Group on Accounting Standards provides assistance to the Committee to monitor the continuing relevance of the chapter on Disclosure of Information and its implementation. In this context, two surveys were conducted in 1987 and 1989 to assess the degree of compliance with the Disclosure of Information Guidelines by multinational enterprises. The 1989 survey is based on the 1987 annual reports of a representative sample of companies in selected Member countries. The sample of companies is largely identical to the one used for the earlier survey, except that forty banks and insurance companies were added. According to preliminary results, no significant changes have taken place since 1987. The Guidelines tend to be more closely followed in those countries where a similar degree of disclosure is required by national rules and practices. However, even in the absence of such rules, the survey noted numerous examples where enterprises voluntarily provided the information called for by the Guidelines, the statement of sources and uses of funds being a case in point.

Disclosure by industrial and commercial enterprises is generally more comprehensive than that by banks and insurance companies although account must be taken of the different nature of their respective activities and of the specific accounting and reporting rules to which the financial services sector is subject. A high level of conformity was found for the following items – structure of the enterprise, geographical areas, sales, sources and uses of funds, accounting methods and consolidation policies. An average level of conformity was found for the items on operating results, new capital investments and average number of employees. While information on these items was generally disclosed, many companies did not provide that information by lines of business and/or geographical areas. Two items showed low compliance – research and development expenditure and intra-group pricing policies.

The results of the survey show that promotional efforts to increase awareness of the Guidelines should be continued and intensified. Further clarifications of the Guidelines may also be needed in order to facilitate compliance. As knowledge and understanding of the Guidelines becomes more widespread, it is expected that compliance with the disclosure recommendation will further improve. The close association of BIAC, TUAC and the international accounting profession to the activities of the Working Group on Accounting Standards has already shown positive results in this direction.

Transparency of the activities of multinational enterprises depends not only on the volume but also on the quality and comparability of the information provided. For this reason, efforts towards increased harmonization of accounting practices are of crucial importance. Since 1984, the Committee, through the Working Group on Accounting Standards, has carried out several studies to promote harmonization in areas of particular relevance to international accounting and reporting.

The active participation of the private sector and the accounting profession contributed to the success of two international conferences organised by the Working Group on Accounting Standards: a Forum on International Harmonization of Accounting Standards was held in 1985 and, in 1988, a Symposium on New Financial Instruments was organised in co-operation with the Committee on Financial Markets. These events provided the occasion for Delegates to follow the main developments in international accounting. The 1985 Forum was also the first opportunity offered to participants from widely different spheres to establish contacts for further co-operation at the international level. The Forum also increased its awareness of the need to take into account the rules already existing before adopting national standards.

In 1988 a Symposium was organised to evaluate the accounting and reporting issues arising from new financial instruments, given their economic importance and implications both for banks and non-banking enterprises. The expansion in transactions has been substantial world-wide, and the movement has gained enormous momentum in recent years. Since the 1970s, agents have been striving to hedge, first against exchange rate volatility and then against interest rate volatility. Initially, new financial instruments were only used by the major financial institutions; they are now accessible to large and medium-sized non-financial institutions. As a result of progress in telecommunications and computer technology, the interconnecting nature of markets and the standardisation of instruments, trading activities can be conducted round the clock in specialised markets across the globe. Major changes in the functioning of financial markets and in the management of risk have far-reaching implications for the efficiency, stability and equity of the financial system and the risk profile, performance and future prospects of enterprises. However, there is no coherent framework for disclosure in financial statements which would meet the needs of the users of these statements. Many of the new instruments are off-balance-sheet and often remain undisclosed.

In reviewing the results of the 1988 Symposium and the subsequent discussion of the Working Group on Accounting Standards, the Committee concluded that the chapter of the Guidelines on Disclosure of Information is comprehensive and flexible enough to deal with the disclosure and accounting issues arising from new financial instruments. These Guidelines indicate a general objective of disclosure of information which is to increase transparency of the structure, policies and activities of multinational enterprises. The Committee also recalled that the list of specific information items set out in the chapter is illustrative and non-exclusive. It therefore covers disclosure of significant off-balance-sheet risks associated with new financial instruments.

The Committee, through its Working Group on Accounting Standards, will continue to examine whether more specific guidance in the form of clarification is needed to indicate to enterprises, both bank and non-financial enterprises, how to improve disclosure of information on new financial instruments in conformity with the Guidelines. In addition, efforts will be made to promote harmonisation of accounting practices in this area.

The provision of information to representatives of employees on a true and fair view of the performance of the enterprise as a whole

While the Disclosure of Information Guidelines address the provision of information to the general public, the Committee stated in the 1984 Review Report that employees of multinational enterprises may need and should have access to more specific information, suitable for their interests and purposes, than that available to the public at large. When this matter was considered in the 1984 Review Report, the Committee stated that certain activities of multinational enterprises such as restructuring activities, may be understood and put into perspective only if the information on the position of the enterprise as a whole is available. It went on to say that if restructuring or similar decisions result in negotiations where the performance of the enterprise as a whole is a key element, then employee representatives should have information which gives a true and fair view of the enterprise as a whole in these instances where, and inasmuch as, such information is needed for meaningful negotiation on conditions of employment.

Particularly paragraphs 2b) and 3 of the Employment and Industrial Relations Guidelines deal with such matters. Paragraph 2b) addresses the information needed for meaningful negotiations on conditions of employment and paragraph 3 is concerned with the provision of information to enable representatives of employees, where this accords with local law and practice, to obtain a true and fair view of the performance of the entity and, where appropriate, the enterprise as a whole. The Committee has held a number of discussions on the intentions of the Guidelines with respect to the provision of information to representatives of employees. In the present Review period, it has focused on the provisions of paragraph 3 of the Employment and Industrial Relations Guidelines and in particular how the notion in that paragraph of "information enabling a true and fair view of the performance of the enterprise as a whole" should be understood.

As a first step in this discussion, the Committee studied the laws, regulations and practices in Member countries, with respect to the provision of information by enterprises to employees. In some countries, there are very extensive and detailed statutory provisions, whereas in others, it is the task of management and labour representatives to define on the basis of needs, the nature of the information which management is expected to provide on a "good faith" basis. Looking across the spectrum of situations in Member countries, there is clearly no general approach to this question; indeed, differences in approaches often appear more pronounced than similarities. This diversity is illustrated by differences in many facets of information provision including the type of information to be provided (e.g. information on the legal situation and structure of the company, investment, production, personnel, financial structure, etc.) and its level of detail, whether it is to be provided at the level of the individual entity or the group (national or international), the timing of the provision (regular, on request, in respect of specific events), whether it covers the present situation and past developments and/or future outlook and the situations in which the information is to be provided (e.g. for general information, for collective bargaining needs, in respect of particular operations, such as closure, restructuring, new technologies, etc.).

In light of the above, and in response to proposals to clarify and present greater detail on the provisions of paragraph 3 of the Employment and Industrial Relations Guidelines, the Committee first reaffirmed its view, already expressed in the 1979 Review Report, that an exhaustive and detailed list of items which would be covered by the expression "information enabling a true and fair view of the performance of the entity and, where appropriate the enterprise as a whole" would neither be feasible nor practical as a result of the diversity in Member country situations.

In discussing these issues, the Committee recalled its opinion, expressed in the 1984 Review Report, that employees may need and should have access to information, beyond that provided to the general public, specific to and suitable for their needs and purposes. With this in mind, enterprises should provide information on key aspects of the performance of the enterprise which will also enable users to assess, inter alia, likely future developments. In so doing, they should be guided, in the first instance, by the information items enumerated in the Disclosure of Information Guidelines. Where more specific information is necessary, management and labour should be prepared to discuss information requirements in a constructive manner, taking account of the specific situation of the enterprise and of local laws, regulations and practices. The Committee is also aware that considerations of business confidentiality may mean that information on certain points may not be provided, or may not be provided without safeguards.

Interlinked enterprises

On the basis of a question raised by TUAC, the Committee discussed the issue of the application of the Guidelines to enterprises or entities located in different countries among which there may be various kinds of links. This issue hinges on the question of what constitutes a multinational enterprise in the sense of the Guidelines. This topic is addressed by paragraph 8 of the Introduction to the Guidelines, which states that "multinational enterprises usually comprise companies or other entities whose ownership is private, state or mixed, established in different countries and so linked that one or more of them may be able to exercise a significant influence over the activities of others and, in particular, to share knowledge and resources with the others." Thus the Guidelines adopt a flexible approach, enumerating some guiding criteria rather than a precise definition of a multinational enterprise which would fit less well the diversity of situations found in the real world.

In relation to the specific questions raised by TUAC, the Committee stated that it is not its intention to change its position, as reflected in the text of the Guidelines, that for the purposes of the Guidelines, no precise definition of a multinational enterprise is required. The Committee further considered that the sharing of knowledge and resources among companies or other entities would not be in itself, i.e., in the absence of other relevant circumstances, a sufficient indication that such companies or entities constitute a multinational enterprise.

In responding to TUAC, the Committee further recalled the provision of paragraph 9 of the Introduction to the Guidelines, which state that the Guidelines reflect good practice for all multinational, and whenever relevant, domestic enterprises and that this principle applies all the more where the enterprises concerned present certain multinational features.

The application of the Guidelines to situations of enterprise closure

Following the abrupt closure of a foreign-controlled enterprise in a Member country, the Committee was requested by the country concerned to address matters related to the Guidelines in the light of that event. In responding to the request, the Committee emphasised a number of points concerning the promotion of the Guidelines, the consideration by enterprises of the policy objectives of Member countries and the provision of reasonable notice in considering changes in operations which would have major effects on the livelihood of their employees, in particular in the case of the closure of an entity involving collective lay-offs or dismissals.

The recommendations to enterprises in paragraphs 1 and 2 of the General Policies chapter of the Guidelines with respect to the established general policy objectives of Member countries and their aims and priorities with regard to economic and social progress apply to all aspects and situations of the operations of enterprises addressed by the Guidelines. The Committee is of the view that these provisions should be borne in mind when, inter alia, enterprises are considering changes in their operations which would have major effects upon the livelihood of their employees, in particular in the case of the closure of an entity involving collective lay-offs or dismissals, which is the subject of paragraph 6 of the Employment and Industrial Relations Guidelines. Indeed, the Committee recalled its statement in the 1984 Review Report that when major restructuring activities are carried out across national boundaries, the Guidelines, for example paragraph 2 of the General Policies chapter, may provide guidance to multinational enterprises as to how they should take into account the interests of the countries in which they operate.

Specific cases have shown that these provisions are of particular relevance when a local subsidiary of a multinational enterprise is to be closed down. In this context, a company should seek all necessary information on the country's relevant aims and practices from the government concerned. The Committee maintains the view that paragraphs 1 and 2 of this chapter of the Guidelines do not affect the right of the enterprise to reach decisions with respect to cutting back or terminating operations in a given plant. But they indicate certain considerations which should be given due weight in making such a decision. If a firm does proceed in this manner, then it clearly follows that the nature of the final decision will be influenced by the considerations set out in paragraphs 1 and 2 whilst respecting the firm's own judgement.

Paragraph 6 of the Employment and Industrial Relations Guidelines addresses the issue of "reasonable notice" and, in the context of the request of the Member country concerned, the Committee emphasised a number of points already made in past discussions of this provision. The key notions are the "reasonable notice" to be given of such changes and actions by management and co-operation with employee representatives and appropriate governmental authorities "so as to mitigate to the maximum extent practicable adverse effects." There is a link between these two notions. The notice given has to be sufficiently timely for the purpose of mitigating action to be prepared and put into effect; otherwise, it would not meet the criterion of "reasonable". It would be in conformity with the general intention of this paragraph, in the light of the specific circumstances of each case, if management were able to provide such notice prior to the final decision being taken. The Committee has emphasised this view on a number of occasions including, for example, in the clarification reported in the sub-section above on employee representation and reasonable notice, in respect of a specific issue concerning "reasonable notice".

The Committee also examined whether further guidance could be provided to enterprises via a further clarification. In the light of the above and its previous clarifications of the Guidelines in respect of the situation addressed, the Committee concluded that the provisions of the Guidelines in respect of the issues raised were sufficiently clear and comprehensive to permit enterprises to proceed in a manner which would be in conformity with the expectations of Member countries as set out in the Guidelines. In noting that the matter in question was eventually settled between management and labour, the Committee felt that the force of the Guidelines added to other pressures on the enterprise concerned to reach, in the end, a satisfactory solution.

Organisational structures of multinational enterprises

The way in which multinational enterprises organise their activities across national frontiers and the relationships between parent and subsidiary enterprises raise important issues for those involved or associated with such decisions. To what extent or in what areas are decision-making structures becoming more centralised or decentralised? More generally, to what extent can the component entities of multinational enterprises have sufficient autonomy and responsibility to permit their integration into the economic context of the countries in which they operate and develop their competitive potential without impinging on the ability of the enterprise to take a global view of the company as a whole with respect to efficiency, competitiveness and profitability?

The Guidelines address a number of recommendations to enterprises which are pertinent to these issues (for example, paragraph 5 of the General Policies chapter), and the way enterprises are structured may be relevant to the manner in which they can follow these recommendations. Naturally, they do not call for the freezing of the structures of multinational enterprises nor do they infringe on the freedom of enterprises to take particular decisions in the furtherance of global strategies judged to be in the best interests of the firm as a whole, but they do contain a number of provisions relevant to this topic. The Committee therefore decided to undertake a study of recent developments in this area in the context of its general aim of ensuring the continued relevance of the Guidelines to changing situations. The results of this work, summarised in the paragraphs below has been published as *Structure and Organisation of Multinational Enterprises* in 1987.

A large variety of factors affect the organisational structures chosen by multinational enterprises and the position of the subsidiary in the enterprise as a whole. One set concerns characteristics of the corporation, such as those related to the parent or group as a whole (e.g., sector, nationality, size, degree of internationalisation, corporate strategy), to specific features of the subsidiary (e.g., country of location, size, age, performance), or to the nature of links (ownership, interdependence) between parent and subsidiary. The other main set of factors concerns the environment in which the enterprise operates, including the economic situation (e.g., market situation, uncertainty and instability), competition, technology (e.g., the role of advanced information technology in facilitating the adoption of a given organisational structure) and the role of host government policies (particularly as they address the position of local subsidiaries via preconditions and/or performance requirements). Outside these two broad sets of forces, the role played by more intangible aspects such as tradition, business philosophy and personalities should not be under emphasised.

It is evident that organisational structures and parent-subsidiary relationships in multinational enterprises, influenced as they are by a large variety of forces, are often complex and fluid. The position of subsidiaries, especially foreign located subsidiaries with respect to the level of decision making authority, is often discussed in the context of the need for supervision and flexibility. Supervision, often associated with more centralised control, is required in large and complex enterprises to ensure co-ordination of activities and the compatibility of subsidiaries' activities with overall company strategy. Flexibility, generally associated with decentralised decision making, concerns the need for appropriate and often rapid actions to meet changing circumstances, where knowledge and experience of the local situation are normally key requirements. The organisational structures of multinational enterprises can be seen as the means by which such enterprises manage these often competing forces.

The exercise of parent authority over a subsidiary's activities may range from direct instruction to passive ratification, while the desired level of oversight of activities can be achieved in various ways such as the use of financial thresholds, production specifications and standardised methods. More indirect means may include the positioning of key personnel and the use of intra-company visits. In the end, however, the question of how management at different levels of the organisational structure interacts, particularly with respect to strategic decisions, may be more important than that of whether the parent or the subsidiary takes a particular decision.

One aspect that stands out in decision making patterns is the distinction between strategic decisions, with a generally high level of parent involvement, and operational decisions, usually associated with high levels of subsidiary decision making authority. Within this broad pattern there are, of course, important differences between multinational enterprises with respect to the degree of centralisation of a particular decision area and how this is achieved. In addition, strategic and operational decisions are frequently linked in that, for example, major capital expenditure decisions such as opening a new plant or undertaking a large expansion affect operational decisions such as employment levels. Thus, while central control in one decision area does not imply similar control in a different area, this must be seen in the perspective of the links that exist between different decision areas.

As the forces affecting organisational structure and patterns change over time, and many of them have changed quite dramatically over the last decade or so, it can be expected that these will be associated with changes in what is felt to be the most suitable organisational form. Clearly, and given the diversity in multinational enterprises with respect to their internal features and the nature of their market situations, changes in organisational structure in any one single direction cannot be expected.

On the basis of this work, the Committee examined possible implications of the issues involved for the Guidelines. This discussion focused on the provision of information on organisational structures to the general public (item 1 of the Disclosure of Information chapter) and to employees (paragraph 3 of the Employment and Industrial Relations Guidelines), and on the freedom of entities to develop their activities and exploit competitive advantage (paragraph 5 and relevant parts of paragraphs 1, 2 and 4 of the General Policies chapter).

In these discussions, the Committee first recalled the clarification issued on the structure of the enterprise in the context of item 1 of the Disclosure of Information chapter which is included in the 1988 publication, *Multinational Enterprises and Disclosure of Information: Clarification of the OECD Guidelines*. In arriving at this clarification, the objective of this chapter was recalled – namely to give greater transparency to the structure, activities and policies of the enterprise as a whole to the general public. Given the description of a multinational enterprise in paragraph 8 of the Introduction to the Guidelines, which covers a broad range of structural patterns of multinational activities, the Committee recalled that item 1 of the chapter does not call for disclosure of detailed organisational patterns and the distribution of managerial activities within the enterprise as a whole. The Committee did note that such information may be relevant for specific user groups such as employees and could be a matter for special purpose reports.

In light of the above, the Committee agreed on the following clarification of item 1 of the Disclosure of Information chapter on the structure of the enterprise: The composition of the enterprise as a whole should be described and disclosure made to provide an overview of the linkages between its various entities. This information should be provided with consolidated financial statements or, where these are not issued, by other means e.g., with individual statements of the entity or entities representing the enterprise as a whole.

The relevance of other areas of the Guidelines to the subject of the structure of multinational enterprises have been taken into account when the Committee addressed the topic of the provision of information on the performance of the enterprise as a whole, the results of which have been reported in the above sub-section dealing with true and fair views. In other areas of the Guidelines relevant to issues linked to organisational structure, the Committee concluded that due, inter alia, to the complexity and fluidity in organisational structures and parent-subsidiary relations, the present Guidelines, together with the relevant clarifications already issued, are fully adequate to provide enterprises with guidance that may be required in meeting their recommendations.

Environmental protection

The Review period has witnessed ever increasing public awareness and concern with the protection of the environment. There have been a number of major environmental accidents, the public is developing a better understanding of new environmental problems relating to, for example, climatic change and the ozone layer, and there is a growing commitment on behalf of the governments of Member countries to protect the environment. The report of the World Commission on Environment and Development, *Our Common Future* (the "Brundtland" report), which has been widely discussed in international fora, highlighted the relationship between environmental policies and sustainable development and considered ways and means of further integrating environmental considerations into a broad spectrum of policy areas. In June 1989, the OECD Council at Ministerial level discussed the relationship between environmental concerns and economic decisions. It decided that the OECD will continue to stimulate and support closer co-operation between government and industry to meet the environmental challenges of the 1990s.

Growing concern with the environment has been reflected in the development of policies at the national level. In view of increasing world-wide economic and technological interdependence, environmental protection has also a strong international dimension. Indeed, certain problems of a bilateral, regional or global significance cannot be dealt with adequately within a national context, their solution depending on international co-operation and agreement.

At their inception, the Guidelines recognised this fact, recommending in paragraph 2 of their General Policies section, that enterprises give due consideration to host countries' aims and policies with regard to the protection of the environment. Around the time of the 1984 Review, the Committee devoted considerable attention to this issue and in 1985, in response to a mandate given to it by the OECD Council, adopted a clarification of the reference to environmental protection in the Guidelines. In so doing, the Committee noted that the period ahead would provide valuable experience of the operation of the Guidelines in the area of environment with the benefit of the clarification and that it would draw on that experience in reconsidering, in the framework of the present Review, whether there is need for further clarification of the Guidelines or for a possible chapter on environment.

The Committee considered this matter in close co-operation with the OECD's Environment Committee and has held a number of consultations with BIAC and TUAC. As a result of its deliberations, the Committee agreed to recommend the introduction of a new chapter in the Guidelines on the subject of environmental protection. This chapter, which is addressed to all enterprises, whether domestic or multinational, privately owned or state owned, is closely based on the clarification issued in 1985 and it should be seen in conjunction with the numerous OECD instruments dealing with the protection of the environment. The text, which can be found in Annex I below, was adopted by the Council in its meeting at Ministerial level on 4-5 June 1991.

The decision to introduce a new chapter was based on a number of considerations. The Committee was of the view that a separate chapter would have a higher visibility than the previous clarification and would be more indicative of the significance given to environmental concerns by Member countries. The introduction of such a chapter recognises the links between economic and environmental objectives and is also seen by the Committee as a concrete reflection of the evolution of environmental awareness in industry. Indeed, the climate and tone of industry-government relationships in the area of environment has evolved notably and increasingly provides an example for co-operation. The International Chamber of Commerce's Environmental Guidelines for World Industry, mentioned above, which were revised in 1986 and supplemented in 1990, recognise that concerted efforts are needed by all to deal with environmental issues, including those related to hazardous wastes. In 1989, the ICC also lent its support to environmental auditing as an internal management tool. International industry's co-operation with governmental and intergovernmental bodies has been steadily increasing in recognition of mutual areas of concern and the desire jointly to address and find practical ways of solving the major international environmental issues. It is against this background that the Committee decided to recommend the introduction of this new chapter in the Guidelines on environmental protection.

The Committee has noted that concerns about the protection of the environment are of a general nature and are not, therefore, limited to the actions of enterprises. This is all the more evident today given the nature of concerns with the environment and the debate underway since the publication of the ''Brundtland'' Report, which addresses the need, too, for governments to define their economic and development goals within this context. For this reason, the Committee has stressed, in introducing this new chapter, the importance of the role to be played by government and the need to make its aims and objectives as clear, stable and understandable as possible to management and of seeking harmonisation of their environmental policies where valid reasons for differences do not exist. It recommends that these matters be noted in the Ministerial statement associated with the adoption of the new chapter.

In its discussions on this new chapter, the Committee also considered the relationship between good safety and health procedures related to the workplace and the protection of the environment. The introductory clause to the chapter includes a reference to the need to avoid creating environmentally related health problems. The Committee has also recalled that issues concerning safety and health are dealt with in the ILO Tripartite Declaration of Principles concerning Multinational Enterprises and Social Policy and has stated in the past, and takes this opportunity to repeat again, that whenever these Principles refer to the behaviour expected of enterprises, they parallel the OECD Guidelines and do not conflict with them. They can, therefore, be of use in relation to the OECD Guidelines to the extent that they are of a greater degree of elaboration, bearing in mind that the responsibilities for the follow up procedures of the OECD Guidelines and the ILO Declaration are institutionally separate.

The Committee has stressed that the new chapter in the Guidelines dealing with the protection of the environment should not be seen as singling out multinational enterprises for special attention. On the contrary, a key feature of the Guidelines is their non-discriminatory nature. The Guidelines do not make, and should not be seen as making, statements or inferences which could be taken to imply differences in the treatment or behaviour of multinational and domestic enterprises or that particular enterprises should adhere to higher standards – both groups of enterprises are subject to the same expectations with respect to their conduct whenever the Guidelines are relevant to both. For these reasons, the Committee has recalled the provisions of paragraph 9 of the Introduction to the Guidelines in the introductory clause of the new chapter. The Committee recalled the support that multinational enterprises can and do give to the public authorities in this context and that they are generally in the forefront in terms of action in the area of environmental protection, of dissemination of information, in the development of environmentally favourable technologies and products, in the prevention of accidents and in the development of emergency procedures. Furthermore, they are often in this position because of their technological knowledge in the environmental area.

The Committee believes that this chapter will further promote environmental protection and good environmental practices by all enterprises. In the light of the above, the Committee has urged BIAC to use its good offices to ensure the full support of enterprises for these recommendations in line with their spirit and objectives and in so doing, to promote the wide implementation of good environmental practices by all enterprises, whether multinational or domestic.

3.   The role of the guidelines in the period ahead

The Guidelines have demonstrated their continued relevance over a period which has seen major changes in international direct investment patterns and the way in which multinational enterprises organise their activities. They are recognised as providing a now well-established mechanism used by Member countries and multinational enterprises to increase co-operation and resolve difficulties. The experience gained with the Guidelines and their implementation has confirmed that they do provide guidance to enterprises in organising and conducting their activities in a manner which is in conformity with their recommendations.

In the period ahead, the Committee will continue its efforts to promote awareness and implementation of the Guidelines along these lines. It will discuss, together with BIAC and TUAC, how the Guidelines can be better integrated into actual management practice, in order to increase their contribution to management training and improve understanding of public policy concerns. With this in mind, the Committee organised in late 1991 a symposium on the promotion of the Guidelines. The symposium, which responded to a need expressed both by business and labour, as well as by Member countries, aimed to identify new areas and users of the Guidelines to which promotional efforts should be devoted, and considered ways and means to ensure the effective implementation of the Guidelines at the national and international levels.

The Committee will also continue to consider proposals to clarify the Guidelines as the need arises and to undertake the work necessary to ensure their continued relevance to new developments. In doing so it will continue to be guided by the needs of stability, balance and flexibility.

In the light of the major developments now underway in the countries of central and eastern Europe, and in particular in respect of the contribution that foreign direct investment can make to the process of moving to more market oriented economies, the Committee will be examining means of fostering the Guidelines in these countries in order to promote international co-operation in the investment area and to contribute to the development of a sound climate of confidence between investors, local partners and host country governments. The Committee will also be examining this issue in respect of other non-member countries, including the Dynamic Asian Economies.

Clearly, a very important task for the Committee, as well as for Member countries and BIAC and TUAC, is to strengthen efforts in the next period to promote awareness and implementation of the Guidelines. As has been made evident in the discussion in chapter I of pressures or tendencies towards protectionism in the investment field, some of these pressures are based on the sentiment that investment by foreign-controlled enterprises is somehow different from that of domestic enterprises and that their commitment and contribution to the host economy does not match that of their domestic counterparts. Yet it is clear that if foreign-controlled enterprises follow the Guidelines, they will be seen as behaving as good corporate citizens. Thus, observance of the Guidelines provides a strong argument against protectionist pressures in the investment area contributing to mutual confidence by all those concerned by the activities of multinational enterprises, management of the enterprises themselves, employees, home and host governments, and the public at large.

Chapter IV

CONFLICTING REQUIREMENTS

Conflicting requirements imposed by countries on multinational enterprises arise when a country's legislative or legal requirements with extraterritorial reach, conflict with legislation or policies in other countries and affect the operations of entities of multinational enterprises located in these countries. The trend towards increasing economic interdependence between countries tends to amplify the risk of such conflicts, especially in areas where one country's assessment of its national interest or legal necessity runs counter to another country's concept of national sovereignty. Similarly, the globalisation of the activities of multinational enterprises is sometimes perceived as increasing the impact – through conduct abroad – on national economies and as allowing greater possibilities for the avoidance of national laws.

As a result of this globalisation, there is the possibility that some countries may rely on the extraterritorial application of their national laws to regulate economic activities. This does not imply that conflicts will necessarily arise in every case, particularly since bilateral and multilateral agreements between countries concerned can resolve potential disputes. Countries are also demonstrating more prudence with respect to the extraterritorial application of their national laws. However, countries which consider themselves adversely affected by the extraterritorial application of other countries' laws or regulations have enacted statutes to block such application. Seen from the business perspective, this may exacerbate the situation in which a particular multinational enterprise finds itself by sharpening even further the conflict in question. The result is to create a climate of uncertainty in which multinational enterprises may either scale back international operations or hesitate to undertake new ones. At the least, it makes doing business more difficult for enterprises so affected.

Recognising the potentially detrimental effect on the international investment climate, Member countries undertook in the context of the 1976 OECD Declaration, to consult one another and to seek co-operative solutions for problems involving conflicting requirements. Since then, growing concern with problems relating to conflicting requirements led Member countries to agree, in the context of the 1984 Review of the Declaration, to a set of general considerations and practical approaches to be taken into account whenever they consider the adoption, modification or application of laws or regulations which may lead to conflicting requirements being imposed on multinational enterprises. This agreement, which is the first multinational approach of its kind to address such problems in the field of international investment, seeks to avoid placing a foreign-controlled enterprise in a disadvantageous position vis-à-vis its relations with its host country.

The general considerations part of the agreement provides a set of principles which Member countries should take into account when considering legislation with extraterritorial reach. The objective of these general considerations is to prevent situations of conflicting requirements from arising or, at least, minimise the potential for conflict. The practical approaches part of the agreement proposes ways and means at the bilateral and multilateral level, based on notification and consultation, for dealing with problems that may arise.

The Committee agreed that considerable progress had been achieved in reducing the risk and seriousness of conflicts resulting from conflicting requirements, notably through the use of the procedures laid down in the 1984 agreement. The Committee felt that the status of this agreement which had proved its effectiveness should be enhanced by integrating into the 1976 Declaration an additional element dealing with conflicting requirements. The general considerations and practical approaches provisions of the 1984 agreement are to be attached to that Declaration in the same way as the Guidelines. Accordingly, a separate Council Decision on Conflicting Requirements which takes up the language of the Second Council Decision on the Guidelines relating to conflicting requirements, was recommended by the Committee and adopted by the Council in June 1991. The substance of the 1984 agreement remains, therefore, unchanged but the amendment of the 1976 Declaration and the adoption of a new Council Decision on Conflicting Requirements gives it the same standing as the other elements of the Declaration. The text can be found in Annexes 1 and 2.

This chapter reviews the work of the Committee, first in identifying and understanding the sources, scope and trends of conflicting requirements, and second, in facilitating international co-operation through the mechanisms provided by the 1984 agreement. Experience gained in implementing the agreement reveals, as already noted above, an improvement as concerns conflicting requirements imposed on multinational enterprises. This is also due to a better mutual understanding of the legitimate needs and interests of both those Member countries affected by the extraterritorial reach of legislation, as well as those countries applying their laws extraterritorially.

1. Sources, scope and trends of conflicting requirements

Given the relatively recent character of the Committee's agreement on conflicting requirements, one of its initial tasks was to obtain a better understanding of why these conflicts arise, the areas in which they are most prevalent, and how an increase in such conflicts could impact on the climate for international direct investment. The Committee has therefore devoted considerable effort to identifying and defining the sources, scope and trends of conflicting requirements.

Sources

In general, the principal sources of conflicting requirements are interventions by governments, on the national or international level, reflecting domestic concerns of a regulatory nature or a desire to enforce national policies. Conflicts can emanate either from extraterritorial legislation or regulations meant to address national economic priorities (taxation, banking, securities regulations, competition, civil aviation and shipping, etc.) or from extraterritorial legislation or regulations taken to meet predominately political concerns (national security interests, foreign policy, etc.). These legal or regulatory requirements may impose specific types of behaviour on enterprises or may forbid other types of behaviour.

An entity of an enterprise established in an OECD country is subject to the legislation and regulations of the country in which it operates and is expected to be responsive to the policies of its host country. Thus, the extraterritorial application of national laws may result in various entities of the same multinational enterprise being subject to different legislation. While this gives rise to divergent influences on some of the entities of a firm, what is of real concern is the situation where various national legislations or regulations impose different requirements on the same entity.

This problem is aggravated by the fact that, traditionally, countries' justifications for these interventions may be based on different legal principles or economic philosophies. Among these principles, territoriality – or the limitation of jurisdiction to strict national boundaries – is one of the principal basis on which state jurisdiction can be founded under international law. Citing, for example, the complexities of a global economy, some countries do not accept this principle as the sole legitimate basis for exercising jurisdiction which purports to regulate economic behaviour. For example, the ''effects'' principle which attempts to regulate foreign conduct that has certain effects on the national economy, has given rise to well-known instances of conflicting requirements whenever the assertion of jurisdiction based on this principle has run counter to claims of sovereignty.

In addition, in times of war or other national security crisis, a state may determine that its interests require an extraterritorial application of economic sanctions or trade embargoes based on a connection, defined in the relevant legislation, between a foreign enterprise and nationals of the regulating state. The use of the nationality principle beyond that which is generally attributed to this principle, to attach legal consequences to foreign corporations in respect of their conduct abroad has given rise to serious incidences of conflicting requirements and is strongly contested by some countries.

To counteract the reach of extraterritorial legislation, many countries have sought to prevent the application of such legislation in their territories. At least twenty countries have already adopted blocking statutes. As most of these are directed against measures taken by another country attempting to impose sanctions extraterritorially or to impel a particular action (enforcement jurisdiction), these statutes may add to the conflict in which a multinational enterprise finds itself. The multinational is put clearly in the position of contravening either of two conflicting requirements. This can happen, for example, when export or foreign assets controls imposed on foreign subsidiaries conflict with the requirements of local laws or policies. It can also occur when a multinational firm is required by its home country to produce documents located abroad whose disclosure is expressly prohibited by foreign blocking statutes.

The international business community is of course concerned with the impact on investment and trading decisions which may result from the situations described above. Even where the conflict is not so clear cut, business organisations have noted that multinational enterprises are forced to find ways of accommodating potential conflicts, and it is evident that this maybe easier for some multinational enterprises than for others. Extraterritorial controls may also harm the competitive position of nationals of the country imposing such controls by making other governments wary of transactions between their nationals and companies of the offending state. The same uncertainties and uneasiness that affect the individual multinational enterprise can have wider negative repercussions on the overall international investment climate.

Whereas it is universally accepted that a state may not attempt enforcement jurisdiction in the territory of another state without consent, there is no similar consensus with regard to a state's jurisdiction to prescribe (legislative jurisdiction). Because of this, efforts have concentrated in recent years on finding solutions which can minimise these conflicts. These efforts include in particular, those of the OECD's 1984 agreement on conflicting requirements. This agreement explicitly excludes those aspects of restrictive business practices which are specifically addressed by the 1986 OECD Revised Recommendation Concerning Co-operation Between Member Countries on Restrictive Business Practices Affecting International Trade.

Scope

As can be seen from the above, conflicts due to the extraterritorial application of national law fall into two principal categories. The first involves measures with extraterritorial reach which are taken to meet economic regulatory objectives. The second category includes conflicts which arise as a result of legislation or regulations taken for other objectives, such as national security interests, foreign policy, emergency war powers, etc.

Extraterritorial legislation taken for internal economic objectives

In areas such as taxation, banking and securities regulations, taking part in an international market in a host country entails a submission by foreign-controlled enterprises to specific laws or regulations of the host country. When these laws or regulations have an extraterritorial reach, i.e., for instance concern the activities of the foreign-controlled enterprise outside the host country, this may lead to conflict with the laws and regulations, and policies of the country where these activities take place.

In banking, for example, it became increasingly evident that there was a need for co-ordinated international action between central banks in their role of prudential supervision of deposit-taking institutions, if overlapping and conflicting requirements on banks were to be avoided. This led to an international agreement, known as the Basle Concordat, adopted in 1979, laying down certain principles of prudential supervision which go a long way to reducing the extraterritorial aspects of such functions and the potential for conflict through discussions with regulatory authorities on extraterritorial aspects.

The area of securities regulation, disclosure of information and other company laws and regulations is one where conflicts caused by the extraterritorial application of national regulatory laws frequently occur. These can arise from the extension, in certain circumstances, of national laws to companies not listed within the jurisdiction, the application of national disclosure laws to foreign-related entities of multinational enterprises carrying on business within a particular jurisdiction, and the use of national investigatory powers against foreign parent companies whose subsidiaries carry on business within the jurisdiction and vice-versa. Such application is usually based on the concerns of the regulating state to protect domestic purchasers and markets from improper security transactions. In the absence of appropriate and agreed international principles and procedures for obtaining information, there is potential for conflict with the policy objectives of other countries.

National competition laws and regulations applied to conduct abroad have given rise to many important instances of conflicting requirements. Although there remain divergent philosophies as to the expediency of regulating certain economic behaviour, increasing international co-operation, as evidenced by the OECD Revised Recommendation concerning co-operation on restrictive business practices mentioned above, and growing acceptance of antitrust objectives, have considerably lessened actual conflicts in recent years.

The extraterritorial application of laws in the area of taxation may reflect the desire of a country to prevent the avoidance or evasion of national taxation laws. However, the remedies to this problem may in some cases lead to the imposition of double taxation. Bilateral agreements, which in most instances are based on the OECD Model Double Taxation Convention on Income and Capital, have avoided or considerably reduced this problem. These agreements have also facilitated the exchange of information in cases of suspected tax avoidance. Co-operation between tax authorities has also helped to resolve, to a great extent, other problems related to the application of unitary taxation principles.

Extraterritorial legislation taken for other purposes

As already indicated, the extraterritorial application of laws and regulations taken for other than internal economic objectives can lead to situations of conflicting requirements. Legislation and regulations in this respect commonly take the form of controls on assets, trade sanctions, export controls and investment prohibitions. Countries imposing such regulations may consider that important national concerns are at stake and they believe this factor to be determinant in cases where extraterritorial application of those laws may cause international conflicts.

During times of war or other national emergencies, countries have often resorted to the imposition of economic sanctions which can include the freezing of assets of the adversary country or a banning of exports of strategic goods. The right of a nation to take such action in time of war does not in itself give rise to much controversy. On the other hand, concern is raised when this type of legislation or regulation is applied with extraterritorial reach, affecting nations which are otherwise neutral in the dispute, and when they are extended to non-crisis periods, becoming applicable on a quasi-permanent basis.

The 1950s, 60s and 70s witnessed a wide range of economic sanctions as a reaction by some countries, including the United States, to political events in others. Some of these sanctions were used to control transactions between US companies, including their foreign subsidiaries, and any designated national enemy. Other US laws restricted foreign corporate entities not on the basis of their US ownership or control, but rather with respect to commercial activities involving US origin goods or technical data.

Whatever the statutory basis, extraterritorial applications of economic sanctions and trade embargoes have given rise to several important instances of conflicting requirements. Such conflicts were particularly serious for the companies concerned where extraterritorial measures were to be applied retroactively, interfering with existing contractual obligations. As a result, subsidiaries of multinational enterprises were confronted with the possible imposition of administrative sanctions by the home country of the parent company if they did not comply with certain instructions and were compelled, at the same time by the local country, to carry on the activity in question. Conflicting obligations have also been significant in situations where orders freezing foreign assets conflict with the legal requirements of the host government. In these instances, the multinational enterprise, by running afoul of one or the other legal requirements, incurs the risk of criminal and civil liability which can act as a strong deterrent to doing business in a particular country. This has led some multinationals to refuse business relations with companies incorporated in countries applying extraterritorial controls.

More recently, greater attention is being paid to curtail extraterritorial application as concerns the imposition of foreign policy controls. Many countries also show restraint in formulating legislation which prohibits investment in particular countries by limiting the extraterritorial reach of such legislation. However, the situations in which conflicting requirements have occurred illustrate the importance that nations attach to regulating activities which may threaten their perceived economic or security interests, as well as sensitivities relating to the protection of a country's sovereign interests. By encouraging early notification and consultation on issues relating to conflicting requirements, the OECD's 1984 agreement aims at reducing the frequency and significance of such conflicts.

Trends

Increasing interdependence in the international economy is a major reason why conduct abroad has a growing impact on national economies; likewise, the possibilities of avoiding national laws are perceived as greater. In order to avoid or minimise conflicts which could arise as a result of this evolution, Member countries are demonstrating increasing willingness to apply moderation and restraint in exercising jurisdiction. International co-operation, based on such instruments as the 1984 agreement on conflicting requirements has contributed to a growing awareness of the sovereign interests of the countries affected by extraterritorial application of legislation. Countries so affected are also better able to appreciate the motivations underlying the extraterritorial reach of certain national laws.

Moderation and restraint is beginning to weigh more in areas involving trade sanctions and export controls designed to achieve political ends. The Committee, in the context of its consultations on conflicting requirements, has been encouraged by the efforts of several countries to avoid or minimise conflicts in this area. Trade restrictions have been narrowed for example in some instances, to reach foreign branches of US companies but not foreign subsidiaries (unless the transaction involves US origin goods or technology). There have also been encouraging precedents in fields such as banking supervision, international transborder data flows and anti-fraud regulations, which suggest the effectiveness of international co-operation. In these areas, conflicts have been minimised in large part due either to international agreements concluded such as the Basle Concordat or to the harmonization of national rules promoted by such actions as the 1985 OECD Declaration on Transborder Data Flows or to a general consensus that certain conduct i.e., fraudulent, should be penalised.

Although there has been progress in minimising conflicting requirements, it remains relatively fragile. For this reason, continuing efforts to consolidate and further develop this progress are necessary.

2. Implementing the 1984 agreement on conflicting requirements

Issues relating to conflicting requirements had already been recognised in the 1976 Declaration and Decisions. Growing concern with the disincentive effects of conflicting requirements on international investment led the OECD in 1984 to adopt a stronger multilateral framework for minimising such conflicts. The 1984 agreement on general considerations and practical approaches provided opportunities for notification, information and consultation among Member countries concerned with national laws that might create conflicting requirements being imposed on multinational enterprises.

Since the adoption of the 1984 agreement, the Committee's work has focused on developing a better understanding among Member countries of the intentions of the general considerations part of the agreement and on how its associated practical approaches may best be implemented. The work of the Committee in these two broad areas, described below, has allowed a better identification of the problems involved, has served to clarify the 1984 agreement itself and has provided a better understanding of where the real problem areas are and the possible solutions.

General Considerations

Moderation and restraint

The 1984 agreement on conflicting requirements provides guidance to Member countries as to general considerations to be taken into account when contemplating new legislation, acting under existing legislation or otherwise exercising jurisdiction in a way which may conflict with the legal requirements or established policies of another Member country and lead to conflicting requirements being imposed on multinational enterprises. One of these considerations is that Member countries concerned should: "endeavour to avoid or minimise such conflicts and the problems to which they give rise by following an approach of moderation and restraint, respecting and accommodating the interests of other Member countries". An initial area addressed by the Committee was countries' understanding of the approach of "moderation and restraint", in order to identify their views on this provision and to consider suggestions as to how such an approach could be made most effective.

The results, published in the 1987 report *Minimising Conflicting Requirements: Approaches of Moderation and Restraint,* examines Member countries' positions with regard to the provision and includes their views on the general nature of the concept of following an approach of moderation and restraint, that is, the conceptual basis or motivation for exercising moderation and restraint. On this point, countries expressed various opinions on whether an approach of moderation and restraint was derived from mandatory rules of international law or from a discretionary political doctrine similar to or encompassing the concept of international comity. This divergence has implications for how the approach of moderation and restraint is applied. For those countries which viewed moderation and restraint as a legal principle deriving from rules of international law, the approach is applied on a systematic basis in accordance with those principles, i.e., automatically. Where the approach is considered discretionary, application is on an ad hoc basis, after a determination of relevant interests. Whatever approach they take on this matter of principle, Member countries agree that each branch of government has a role to play in following an approach of moderation and restraint.

As concerns the application of the approach by Member countries in relation to domestic laws, policies and practices, the report looks at the general practices of the executive, legislative and judicial branches of Member countries. In the exercise of their prescriptive jurisdiction, some Member countries noted the careful formulation of legislative proposals by the executive branch in order to avoid or minimise potential conflicts. Bilateral law enforcement negotiations, as well as multilateral arrangements were also devices used by the executive branch to enforce domestic laws or regulations. Concerning practices of the legislative branch, the exercises of self-restraint include limiting the extraterritorial application of statutes and modifying laws with extraterritorial reach to include provisions for notification, consultation and co-operation in relation to their enforcement. The judicial branches also follow a variety of practices for giving recognition to the approach of moderation and restraint in applying and enforcing its domestic laws in cases involving transnational or international elements. In interpreting the extraterritorial application of statutes, for example, some courts will not apply domestic law or exercise jurisdiction over persons or conduct outside their territory. Other courts which do not follow this approach may determine on a case-by-case basis whether and to what degree, in the light of relevant legislation and facts, to exercise restraint in applying domestic laws over persons or conduct outside their territory. They may also adopt a balancing of interests test, or a jurisdictional rule of reason, in cases of concurrent jurisdiction, that gives consideration to a certain number of factors including the interests of other affected states. Some countries questioned, however, whether a court is the proper forum for balancing foreign sovereign interests.

There is also considerable diversity in the application of the approach as concerns the recognition and enforcement of other Member countries' laws, policies or judgements. The bilateral and multilateral approaches adopted at the executive level, discussed above, are generally applicable in this area as well as the exercises of legislative self-restraint. The judicial approach in Member countries relating to the recognition and enforcement of foreign law with extraterritorial reach is in many instances largely determined by statutes. Some countries will give judicial recognition of foreign laws with extraterritorial effect provided such jurisdiction is based on the principle of nationality or the protective principle (i.e., the need to protect vital domestic interests), or where the avoidance of domestic law through the establishment of a foreign company is evident. Foreign judgements are recognised and enforced by the courts of some Member countries on the basis of the principle of comity and reciprocity. Where blocking statutes exist, the court may enforce foreign judgements without requiring reciprocity as long as the restrictions of the blocking statute are not contravened. In looking at requests for judicial assistance, the most frequent approaches concern letters rogatory, as well as the use of bilateral or multilateral arrangements.

In commenting on ways of enhancing moderation and restraint, Member countries agreed on the utility of mutual assistance treaties, as well as bilateral arrangements, in particular with respect to economic regulations (such as export controls), discovery of evidence abroad, and antitrust enforcement. Multilateral consultative mechanisms including the Committee's 1984 agreement on general considerations and practical approaches and the 1986 revised Recommendation on co-operation on restrictive business practices affecting international trade, were cited as particularly relevant for resolving the problems of conflicting requirements.

In summary, the report reveals that there are important areas of agreement and makes more transparent the remaining differences among Member countries' views. The

differences appear to be most pronounced on general topics, e.g., concerning the fundamental nature (legal, political) of approaches to moderation and restraint. Similarities
tend to become more important when implementation is concerned, and more generally
on practical matters such as balancing of competing states' interests, judicial rules of
abstention or deference to foreign law or jurisdiction, etc. The report also emphasises that
international co-operation in the area of conflicting requirements is evolving rapidly. This
implies, in particular, that approaches to moderation and restraint are also evolving,
revealing improved mutual understanding among Member countries achieved in part
through their co-operation in the Organisation in the area of conflicting requirements.

Jurisdictional rule of reason

In the context of its work on the general considerations provisions of the 1984
agreement, the Committee took note of study by the International Chamber of Commerce
(ICC) on *The Extraterritorial Application of National Laws*. That study reviews and
analyses the problems of extraterritoriality from the perspective of international business,
comments on the effects of extraterritoriality on international business and trade, and
proposes certain principles and procedures for resolving extraterritorial problems.

The ICC's study provided an overview of trade and industry experience with the
problems of extraterritoriality in eight industrial regulatory areas, as well as an analysis of
these experiences and their effects. The ICC determined, on the basis of this analysis, that
the extraterritorial application of national laws and policies creates a climate of commercial and legal uncertainty, distorts investment and trading decisions, creates unwarranted
costs and has other adverse effects for international business. It proposed principles for
reducing jurisdictional conflicts resulting from extraterritoriality which includes subject-
ing the extraterritorial application of national laws to a jurisdictional rule of reason. In the
ICC's view, this rule should prohibit unreasonable applications of such laws. Reasonable-
ness should be determined by weighing competing national interests and the need to
facilitate the free flow of international commerce.

In considering this important contribution by the international business community,
the Committee discussed several of its conclusions. As to the proposal regarding the rule
of reason and to the suggestion that the OECD explore the feasibility of establishing a
forum for resolving certain extra-territorial disputes, the Committee decided that although
further consideration of these proposals is not to be excluded, there is clearly not
sufficient international consensus to permit the Committee to endorse them at this time.

Extraterritorial information requirements in securities regulations

Extraterritorial information requirements in the field of securities regulation raises a
number of issues relating to conflicting requirements. Indeed, as already noted, the
growing internationalisation of business and trade in securities, the impact of conduct
abroad on national markets and the possibilities for avoidance of domestic laws has been
increasing. This has led some countries to attempt to control such developments by
adopting laws and regulations that impose disclosure obligations on an extraterritorial
basis and by requiring, as part of their enforcement efforts, the discovery of documents or
testimony located abroad needed to prove violations of these national laws and
regulations.

In order to provide a background for examining these issues the Committee's report,
Extraterritorial Information Requirements in Securities Regulations made available to
the public in 1988, first gives an overview of the general features of Member countries'

principal laws or regulations in the field of securities noting, in particular, major similarities or differences in these laws. Similarities are most apparent in the area of registration requirements including reporting and disclosure requirements in connection with the offering of securities, as well as registration and licensing requirements for brokers and dealers. There is more diversity as concerns the information requirements under these laws or regulations, with fewer legal requirements attaching to the registration of holdings of securities than those pertaining to the disclosure of information in reporting. The report noted that the manner in which Member countries enforce their securities laws or regulations differs in terms of the extent of remedies and sanctions available.

Extraterritorial information requirements in the securities field were examined from the perspective of both requests for information applied extraterritorially as well as the mechanisms by which Member countries grant assistance to foreign authorities seeking disclosure of information for regulatory purposes. A majority of Member countries' securities laws and regulations require (or have the potential to require) disclosures of information relating to enterprises or persons located outside of their territory, and to securities transactions conducted by persons or enterprises located abroad. However, with regard to the enforcement of their securities laws, substantially fewer countries' laws authorise regulatory authorities to request information from sources located abroad for such purposes. Member countries indicated a general willingness to provide some form of assistance to governments or regulatory authorities seeking information for enforcement or regulatory purposes, but this willingness may be subject to certain conditions or requirements such as the existence of a mutual assistance treaty between the two countries concerned. In almost all countries, legal confidentiality requirements, secrecy laws, or blocking statutes impose certain limits on the ability of companies or government authorities to respond to information requests from abroad.

The report also considers the various mechanisms which Member countries currently employ or have proposed to facilitate international exchange of information in the field of securities regulations. These mechanisms include domestic laws or regulations aimed at minimising divergent legal requirements which inhibit international trading of securities, or regulatory and enforcement efforts by domestic authorities, as well as understandings and agreements, bilateral or multilateral, which can be used to obtain assistance in the international exchange of information for regulatory or enforcement efforts in the area of securities.

In providing a general understanding of the differences and similarities in Member countries' regulatory schemes for securities transactions, the report shows where conflicts have and continue to occur. Some countries indicated that there will be a growing need for information located abroad necessary for enforcement purposes due to the increase in international transactions in the securities markets and the ability to conceal evidence of violations outside national territories. The fact that only few Member countries have laws or regulations governing insider trading, may create situations of conflicting requirements where companies are required to disclose information located abroad in enforcement investigations involving accusations of insider trading. As these activities may not be recognised as crimes by the country to which the request is addressed, any existing mutual assistance treaty pertaining to criminal investigations may not apply.

The report also addresses the problems encountered by multinational enterprises in complying with extraterritorial information requests. These included increased costs of multinational listings as a result of divergent disclosure of information requirements, such as prospectus requirements which must be met by companies seeking listings on stock exchanges. Likewise, differences in generally accepted accounting principles can cause problems for multinationals as such differences result in variations in the financial information which must be disclosed as part of overall disclosure requirements. As already seen, problems related to conflicting requirements on multinational enterprises which arise from secrecy or blocking laws can have important consequences on multinational enterprises.

Corporate nationality and international conflicts of jurisdiction

The uncertainty associated with the extraterritorial application of national laws and possible conflicting requirements arising therefrom, have been signalled out as being particularly damaging to investment activities in general. On the level of individual multinational enterprises such conflicts may serve to discourage or reduce particular investment decisions. The 1984 agreement on Conflicting Requirements has contributed to a significant amelioration of this situation, but the Committee recognised that there remain areas where conflicts seem to be particularly acute.

For this reason, the Committee undertook the study of the principle of corporate nationality and its function as a basis for the assessment and exercise of international jurisdiction in the legislative and enforcement areas. In this context, the legal status or behaviour of a corporation may give rise to jurisdictional claims by more than one state. Each of these states claims the existence of a genuine connection between the given corporate status or behaviour and its sovereign interests in prescribing or enforcing its legislation. Because these claims may not be mutually exclusive, a conflict situation may arise in which one state's successful exercise of jurisdiction could result in prejudice to another state's laws and/or policies. A multinational enterprise caught in the middle of this conflict may see its operations adversely affected as a result.

The study focused on one of the principal methods through which national legal orders extend their jurisdictional reach to extraterritorial conduct, i.e., the extension of the concept of nationality. This extension occurs when foreign incorporated affiliates of domestic corporations are treated as nationals for purposes of asserting jurisdiction over them. Legislators and/or courts have, in certain circumstances, disregarded the fact of separate incorporation and the existence of several affiliated legal persons within the same group and treated the whole enterprise as a single economic entity for the purpose of determining its national allegiance.

The use of the concept of nationality as a basis for asserting legislative jurisdiction is widespread in respect to crimes, including economic ones, and offences that relate to national security. Some countries may also attach importance to other interests such as foreign policy, sufficient to require the allegiance of its nationals. Nationality has also served as a basis for the exercise of extraterritorial jurisdiction on many occasions but controversy may arise when a country, in order to regulate extraterritorial conduct, uses the criteria of control to determine the nationality of the corporate body. The problems may be particularly acute when a substantial, connection with the multinational enterprise in question is inferred solely from the controlling interest in the capital of a company incorporated in another country.

These conflicts can take place in the context of regulation of foreign branches of domestic corporations, the regulation of foreign subsidiaries of domestic parents, as well as the regulation of the parent's behaviour towards the foreign subsidiary. In each case, there may be serious risk of conflict between the foreign policy and security interests of the home country and the sovereign interests of the host state. In these circumstances, general limitations in the exercise of jurisdiction such as the 1984 agreement on Conflicting Requirements as well as approaches based on comity have contributed to minimising conflicts and to the exercise of moderation and restraint by national legal systems.

In practice however, there seems to be less controversy on jurisdictional issues in areas where national policies coincide. In certain areas of economic regulation in which piercing of the corporate veil occurs, such as consolidated accounts of MNEs for tax and reporting purposes, conflicts have been limited by the similarities of legislative approaches among Member countries. This consensus is less likely to be present in areas such as export controls indicated by foreign policy objectives, which may provoke disagreement on the suitability of the policies applied or the effectiveness of particular types of measures.

The CIME will continue to discuss the different concepts of corporate nationality with a view to clarifying the position of Member countries and exploring mutually acceptable solutions. In this context, special attention should be given to the principles contained in the 1984 agreement on Conflicting Requirements.

Practical approaches

The objective of the practical approaches provisions of the 1984 agreement is to encourage and assist Member countries in finding suitable approaches for dealing with the problems relating to conflicting requirements.

Bilateral arrangements

The Committee recognises the importance and the contributions made to minimising conflicting requirements through the use of bilateral arrangements in certain circumstances. These arrangements, in accordance with the practical approaches provisions of the agreement, can serve to limit the damaging effects resulting from such conflicts. In general, these arrangements take account of the legitimate need for economic regulation and law enforcement by one country and the sovereignty of the other country and they provide practical solutions for co-operating in areas which raise issues of conflicting requirements. A prominent example is mutual legal assistance treaties that establish a procedure for intergovernmental assistance in obtaining evidence located abroad and needed for criminal law enforcement purposes, such as the treaties concluded between the United States and Canada and the United States and Switzerland. This latter agreement has been complemented by a memorandum of understanding signed on 8th November 1987 which is intended to avoid, or at least reduce as much as possible, conflicting requirements resulting from the adoption of restrictive unilateral measures with extraterritorial effect.

This objective of bilateral co-operative solutions can also be pursued on a more informal level. Thus the United States and Canada have established a working group which meets on an ad hoc basis to review outstanding subpoenas, issued mostly by United States officials, in order to find solutions for facilitating the production of documents for investigations in a manner that satisfies legal requirements. The approach of bilateral agreements, particularly in the area of extraterritorial demands for information has minimised serious conflicts, for example, by eliminating controversy due to differences in discovery principles and procedures.

Another example of the use of bilaterals was reported by the governments of the United States and the United Kingdom which concluded a framework agreement to allow discussions between the two countries on issues relating to the application of US export controls to UK persons with a view to finding ways of minimising the practical problems arising in this area. Arrangements were made for consultations between the two governments if it appeared that problems might arise in relation to the application of US administered export controls to companies or individuals in the UK. They also agreed to consult if the UK government envisaged using blocking action under its Protection of Trading Interests Act, in relation to the application of those controls. These arrangements provided a framework for reaching a more elaborate understanding between the two countries on specific export controls on supercomputers, setting down administrative procedures that avoid the imposition of conflicting requirements.

Information and consultation on a multilateral basis

Bilateral approaches can be quite effective in dealing with precise situations, but they do not take account of the divergent approaches or philosophies among Member countries which can give rise to conflicts in the first instance. Multilateral arrangements therefore not only provide a support to bilateral ones, to which recourse can be made if the latter prove unable to resolve the matter, but they also provide a mechanism for dealing in an effective manner with other questions which can be satisfactorily addressed only in a multilateral framework.

The multilateral elements of the 1984 agreement are centred on provisions concerning notification and consultation. Discussions in the Committee as illustrated below, show how Member countries have been implementing the practical approaches of the agreement.

For example, the United States reported that the government has commenced a process of reviewing the scope of jurisdiction in substantive proposals to ensure that the rights of sovereigns are taken into account. In the trade sanctions imposed on Nicaragua, the regulations were drafted so as to avoid affecting re-exports from third countries. Additionally, in the case of the Commercial Space Launch Act, United States licenses were not required for launches in the territory of a foreign country unless an agreement between the United States and the foreign country required a United States licence.

Information on measures to minimise conflicting requirements was also provided to the Committee by Canada, which has taken steps to promote co-operative solutions to potential or actual issues of conflicting requirements. Canada filed comments on two legislative proposals in the United States – the Securities and Exchange Commission's "waiver by conduct" proposal and a bill then before the United States Senate, "The Foreign Trade Antitrust Improvements Act of 1985". In addition, Canadian officials communicated to the United States' State Department their views that a private antitrust case which was pending before the United States Supreme Court raised the potential for conflict with other countries' laws or established policies, and suggested that the Department bring these foreign relations issues to the attention of the Court.

In notifying the Committee of legislation with potential for conflict under the practical approaches provision of the agreement, some Scandinavian countries reported that the general considerations of the 1984 agreement were taken into account when adopting legislation such as that forbidding investments in South Africa and Namibia. In particular, while the legislation applies in principle to investments by the foreign subsidiaries of these countries, the laws explicitly provide that the prohibitions are not applicable where they would require conduct abroad that is inconsistent with the laws of the country where the conduct occurs.

Other examples of co-operative approaches adopted by the various branches of government were reported by the Federal Republic of Germany and the European Communities. Concerning the ruling in the Rothman/Phillip Morris case imposing limitations on the application of extraterritorial jurisdiction under the effects doctrine, the German government noted that this decision will have a moderating influence on future assertions of extraterritorial jurisdiction, as it has prompted its enforcement officials to consider the international law principles that ordinarily limit the effects doctrine. The European Communities cited the Commission decision in the Market Sharing by Aluminium Producers Case as an example of implementation of the Committee's practical approaches part of the 1984 agreement in that the Commission took into account the interests and practices of other countries in deciding the case.

In addition, notifications and discussions in the Committee on information provided by Member countries improved the scope of understanding on the practical approaches provision; for example the interpretation to be given to the requirement of information to other Member countries as soon as practicable of new or proposed legislation with significant potential for conflict. On the basis of an actual notification by a Member country, the Committee considered the most appropriate interpretation of this provision. Member countries agreed that such legislation should be brought to the attention of the Committee in due time to permit full consideration of its implications. This would allow authorities of the Member country in question to become more familiar with the views and concerns of other Member countries and would thus put them in a better position to take them into account when finalising its proposed legislation or regulations.

The Committee agreed that while the notion of "significant potential" in the understanding on practical approaches is indeed relevant, it would be highly desirable that information on proposed measures be transmitted as soon as possible to the Organisation in case there could be any doubt on the potential for conflicts that could result from these measures. This agreement is also relevant to other provisions calling for consultations with other Member countries.

3. Role of international co-operation in minimising or avoiding conflicting requirements

Due to the innovative character of the 1984 agreement, conceived as a means of addressing the problems relating to conflicting requirements and their effect on multinational enterprises and the investment climate, a considerable amount of initial work was necessary to identify the sources of conflicting requirements. This work has contributed to a better understanding of the problems and a more coherent implementation of the agreement in order to resolve them.

Countries are increasingly aware of the difficulties and negative impact of conflicting requirements imposed on multinational enterprises and they are exercising more restraint in the adoption of legislation or regulations with extraterritorial application. It is also evident that countries affected by such extraterritorial application are demonstrating a more understanding attitude towards the law enforcement concerns of other countries.

While there is growing mutual accommodation of one another's interests, there are still areas of concern. The problems resulting from conflicting national rules which are applied on an extraterritorial basis are more serious in some fields than in others, and this is often due to differences in international co-operation in different areas. The 1984 agreement and the work of the Committee since then has certainly contributed to the progress that has been achieved in avoiding or resolving conflicting requirements. A key task of the Committee in the years ahead is to consolidate this progress, by addressing areas where difficulties continue to exist.

Chapter V

INTERNATIONAL INVESTMENT INCENTIVES AND DISINCENTIVES

In stimulating investment, Member countries rely mainly on macroeconomic policies to set the scene for productive investment in general, with investment incentives being used to provide additional stimulus or guidance for investments in particular areas or directions. Nevertheless, all OECD Member countries employ, to varying degrees, investment incentives measures to promote objectives in a variety of policy areas such as industry and technology, regional policy, service sector activities and small-firm development. Although more restricted in incidence, a number of OECD countries also apply particular measures which may have a disincentive impact on investment, particularly foreign direct investment. Over the last period, however, there has been a general trend towards some reduction in the overall level of government intervention. On the one hand, this is associated with greater efforts by countries to use general economic policies to improve the economic climate, to encourage growth and to reduce uncertainty and instability. There is a greater reliance on the role of the market to guide investment decisions with greater emphasis on attracting foreign investment by the removal or relaxation of restrictions. On the other hand, for investment incentives, there is increasing emphasis in the criteria determining awards and award levels that enterprises demonstrate a need for assistance and that expenditure on assistance demonstrates value for money. Incentives programmes have also been subject to budgetary restraint pressures that have affected government expenditure in all Member countries.

The work of the Committee in the field of international investment and incentives and disincentives is based on of the 1976 Declaration where Member countries recognised the need to strengthen international co-operation on these issues and to take account of Member country interests affected by incentives and disincentives to such investment (see Annex 2). In this connection, Member countries agreed to make such measures as transparent as possible so that their scale and purpose could be easily determined and they set up consultation and review procedures to make co-operation between Member countries more effective in this field.

A considerable part of the Committee's work on investment incentives and disincentives is of an analytical nature, aimed at identifying objectives, trends and effects of incentives and disincentives. As is evident from Chapters I and II, an important part of the efforts of the Committee to remove obstacles to international direct investment is also conducted through its work on the National Treatment instrument.

In the period covered by the Review, the major element of the Committee's work has consisted of updating and developing work published in 1983 under the title

International Investment and Multinational Enterprises: Investment Incentives and Disincentives and the International Investment Process. This led to publication in 1989 of *Investment Incentives and Disincentives and their Effects on International Direct Investment* the main conclusions of which are set out in this chapter. In undertaking this work, the Committee paid particular attention to trade-related investment measures in Member countries and developing countries with a view to assisting Member countries in their preparations for the Uruguay Round of GATT negotiations.

1. Objectives and instruments of incentive and disincentive policies

Scope of the study

An initial task at the outset of the study of incentives and disincentives was to establish definitions of these concepts. In wishing to avoid a rigid or arbitrary definition, the survey took the following approach. An incentive will be understood as any government measure designed to influence an investment decision, or having the effect of increasing the profit accruing to the potential investment or altering the risks attached to it. This definition includes measures which may lead a potential investor to modify a project, even if these measures do not influence directly the profitability of the project as long as they affect the risk involved. It has the advantage of excluding economic factors such as market size, comparative advantage and price stability, or socio-political factors which determine the general context or climate of investment and corresponding general policies. However, it is stressed that the necessary distinction between the measures included in the survey and economic or socio-political factors presents certain difficulties. For instance, measures reducing the rate of taxes on profits in specific sectors in a particular country are to be considered as investment incentives even though the reduced tax rate may be higher than the general rate of taxes on profits in another country. More generally, investment incentive measures are sometimes taken with the purpose of compensating for what are considered as unfavourable influences of economic and socio-political factors. These elements have to be kept in mind, and obviously the role of economic or socio-political factors, which may carry considerable weight in an investment decision, are to be taken into consideration in further analyses, for instance, when assessing the impact and effectiveness of the measures singled out in accordance with the definition used.

Disincentives to international direct investment will be understood as any government measures which are designed to or which have the effect of reducing the profit accruing to the investment or increasing the risks attached to it. While certain measures are clearly taken to limit or exclude investment, particularly foreign direct investment, in particular sectors or activities, others are intended to ensure the achievement of particular goals or objectives, although these measures may clearly have a disincentive or discouragement effect on investment.

To avoid undesirable duplication of efforts and to reduce the scope of the survey in order to make it more specific and operational, some additional categories of measures have been excluded from the present survey. For example, disincentives attached to the authorisation of inward direct investment and/or establishment, including preconditions or performance requirements linked to authorisation of inward direct investment, are excluded. Some measures may nevertheless be discussed occasionally in this chapter when, for example, it is felt that they are of particular relevance. Similarly, obstacles, restrictions or impediments related to investments by foreign-controlled enterprises already established in the host country are generally excluded except where they relate specifically to the incentives and disincentives on which the Committee's survey focused. Trade measures such as export subsidies, etc., are not included in the survey, on the understanding that the possible repercussions on investment of these measures should be part of a complete economic assessment of incentives and disincentives. However, a number of incentives to international investment may be seen as also affecting trade flows, some of these possibly leading to trade distortion. In this sense, the measures in question may be considered as trade-related investment incentive measures. These measures are covered in this report as well as trade-related investment measures which are likely to have disincentive effects on investment.

International investment incentives

Member countries continue to use a wide variety of instruments to stimulate investment. The main categories of measures are fiscal incentives (such as accelerated depreciation, tax rebates, tax exemption etc.), financial incentives (grants, low interest loans, loan guarantees) and non-financial incentives (infrastructure provision, information, advisory and management services). Although there have been changes in the targeting and direction of these measures the incentives measures themselves have nevertheless remained largely unchanged.

Investment incentives are generally available to all investors, regardless of their nationality. There are, however, a small number of measures unavailable to firms under foreign control or which are, on the contrary, intended only for such firms (where the country wants to attract international direct investment). Incentives are administered sometimes at the level of central government and sometimes by state, regional or local authorities. The relative importance of measures taken by central government compared to those introduced at sub-national level depends very largely on the country's institutional set-up. This explains why in many unitary countries central government incentives prevail, whereas in the United States action by individual States predominates. In a third group of countries (such as Germany and France) central and local incentives are both important. In more global terms, tax incentives seem generally to be offered by central government, while financial and non-financial incentives are frequently offered by local or regional bodies when these have independent powers.

Reflecting the fact that Member countries recognise the benefits of international direct investment, outward as well as inward, investors are mostly free to take investment decisions on the basis of commercial criteria and only a few countries place certain controls or limitations on outward investment. However, most countries have taken special steps to promote and assist direct investment in the developing countries, for example by way of tax credits, preferential loans, grants for feasibility studies or to cover insurance of commercial or political risks.

In the developing countries, incentives to attract international direct investment are generally similar those used by Member countries, but there seems to be a preference for fiscal incentives and export processing zones over financial stimulants. Export processing zones in the developing countries are generally designed to attract foreign investment by offering a series of tax advantages and essential infrastructure and the number of such zones has increased considerably over the last period.

Disincentives and preconditions attached to the award of incentives

Investment incentives invariably have conditions of award attached to them. These conditions, which should not be seen as disincentives and which are neither intended to have disincentive effects, generally concern the eligibility, viability and additionality of projects. The broad rationale and objective behind these conditions concern the need to justify public expenditure and to ensure a real benefit from the award of assistance.

Member countries do have a variety of measures which, by design or effect, can have a disincentive effect on inward direct investment, including its initial establishment and/or activities after establishment. Such measures, cover a variety of controls and other impediments such as authorisation procedures, foreign ownership limitations, restrictions on certain modalities of investment or other discriminatory practices whereby invest-ments by foreign-controlled enterprises are treated less favourably than those of their domestic counterparts in various areas including, for example, access to local finance, ability to gain government purchasing contracts, tax treatment, etc. As noted above, such measures, which are generally dealt with under the Capital Movements Code or the National Treatment instrument, were largely excluded from the study. The effects of such measures on investment have been outlined in chapters I and II above.

Special attention was given in the Committee's work over the review period to trade related investment measures (TRIMs), with a view to analysing their effect on interna-tional direct investment. At the same time, such measures were also included in the Uruguay Round of GATT negotiations with the aim of limiting and bringing discipline to their use. A variety of investment measures have been mentioned by participants in the GATT negotiations as having a restricting or distorting effect on trade patterns. These include restrictions or requirements relating to local content, exports, trade-balancing, product mandating, sales and supplies, manufacturing, licensing and technology transfer, local equity, exchange and remittances, and various other restrictions and requirements concerning financing or investment into unrelated areas. The GATT negotiations are continuing and no conclusions have yet been reached on how the GATT disciplines will apply TRIMs, but it is clear from the Committee's own work that whatever the trade effects of individual TRIMs they certainly affect the climate in which international investment decisions are taken. The Committee also recognised that although such measures are used widely in the developing countries, they are also to be found in some Member countries.

One of the main objectives underlying the use of TRIMs, especially in developing countries, is to seek to ensure, if not increase, the benefit to the host economy from direct investment, generally by way of pursuing a higher level of integration with the host economy (e.g., via local content, local ownership, etc. requirements). In certain cases, measures (such as local content or export requirements) are directly intended to result in trade benefits to the host country.

The types of measures listed above may be linked to the award of incentives (for example, the availability or level of a particular award may be conditional upon or in some way proportional to the fulfilment of such requirements or may enter more gener-ally into the assessment of applications for incentives), but in other cases they may be separate from incentives systems. For example, they may arise as a condition imposed at the time of establishment, acquisition or expansion of a direct foreign investment, they may be created when an investor commits to undertake certain activities as a result of negotiations with government authorities concerning the terms under which the investment will take place, or new or expanded TRIMs may be imposed on a firm after the investment has been made, even when there have been no major changes in its characteristics. The latter emphasises a point often made by investors, as illustrated in the report on the Promotion of Private Foreign Direct Investment in Developing Countries, published by the ICC in 1988, that important practical difficulties are also posed by the lack of stability and transparency of measures and that improvement in these areas would make an important contribution to the investment climate.

While the use of measures placing conditions on establishment, acquisition or expansion is generally restricted to investments of foreign-controlled enterprises, in other situations they may apply to both domestic and foreign-controlled enterprises. Even here, however, there may be discriminatory treatment; for example, certain types of incentives measures may be reserved only to domestic enterprises or requirements at higher levels may be imposed on foreign-controlled enterprises.

In the developing countries, most of which apply one and often several of these measures, local content and export requirements are the measures most frequently used. Most performance requirements are general in nature and apply to investments regardless of their sector of activity. Nevertheless, a large number of sector specific measures do exist and are generally concentrated in industries such as automobiles and related production and, to a lesser extent, computers and telecommunications and also in mining, chemicals and the food industry. Sectoral requirements are often quite prevalent in Latin American countries while many Asian countries have numerous and diverse requirements. In Africa, only a few countries impose performance requirements, as much because of a lack of such investment as due to their policy regime for international direct investment.

It is important to underline that the information available does not necessarily provide for a complete or accurate picture of performance requirements in developing countries. The measures discussed above are often, but not always, documented in countries' laws and regulations or policy statements. Often, it is not possible to obtain a clear idea of the ways in which these measures are implemented, for example, whether the measures in question are automatic or discretionary, the extent to which they are applied on a case-by-case basis or their degree of negotiability. In addition, the position is often even more vague, where the language describing the policies includes expressions such that performance requirements are in principle, often or may be required, that there may be some pressure to accept them, or that acceptance may facilitate approval or often attract subsidies. These aspects, together with other features of the information available mean that the discussion of these measures must be rather impressionistic and illustrative of regimes in countries or regions. What is clear, however, is the way such measures are generally perceived by investors. In particular they give a negative impression of the investment climate, not only vis-à-vis foreign direct investment but more generally with respect to private investment and the role to be played by market forces and commercial criteria. It also seems that such negative impressions are not necessarily alleviated when incentives are offered together with performance requirements. Indeed, some investors have reported that they would prefer a situation with no measures to one where disincentives and incentives operate together.

Trends in investment incentives and disincentives

Incentives

While there has not been any broad or general trend in the OECD area either towards major expansion or reduction in expenditure on investment assistance, it does seem that a common approach has been to keep more or less the same armoury of measures but to retarget them to new areas of interest and concern and in order, also, to increase their effectiveness. One general theme which is evident in the increasing use of incentives geared to working with the market mechanism, revealing greater concern with avoiding distortions to investment decisions, as made evident by the switch in some countries from traditional assistance towards market facilitation measures.

In relation to the latter, an important feature of the period covered has been the major fiscal reforms which a number of Member countries have undertaken or are considering. Clearly, the level and structure of business taxation plays an important role in stimulating investment in general and differences between countries may influence international direct investment patterns. In line with the broad trends in OECD countries towards greater reliance on market forces to guide investment decisions as well as towards reduced government intervention, there have been important tax reforms in a number of countries aimed at providing broader based incentives to investment through often considerable reductions in corporation tax schedules. One of the main objectives of these changes is to encourage investment decisions to be based more on business rather than on tax considerations and, in a number of specific examples, certain fiscal incentives have been abolished in the context of the broader changes that have been made to tax regimes.

Another important general feature of changing practices in Member countries is the continuing move from defensive to positive measures. This trend has intensified and spread over the 1980s. Governments have progressively abandoned defensive policies of support for declining industries, it being increasingly accepted that plant closures are inevitable and industrial restructuring essential in economies facing technological innovation and fiercer national and international competition. There has therefore been a continuing shift in emphasis from incentives to maintain enterprises to incentives intended more to stimulate investment in advanced technologies and investment to enhance productivity.

These developments aim to facilitate structural adjustment by stimulating investment in new industrial activities using new technologies such as robotics, new materials, biotechnology, information technology, and in mature industries such as steel, shipbuilding and textiles where the introduction of the new technologies can help structural adjustment. To promote investment in advanced technologies and new industries, government incentives now often favour a horizontal approach so that aid is available to industry as a whole, replacing schemes previously geared to specific sectors.

Certain aids previously limited to manufacturing have also now been extended to cover service activities, with certain specific service sector schemes downgraded or withdrawn as a result. The growth of support for new technology in general is leading governments to encourage high technology services such as telecommunications and computer services, and the development of new financial services.

The eligibility of small enterprises for investment incentives is another feature that has gained prominence in the last years. The main approach has been to inform better small firms that they are eligible for investment incentives and by improving policy delivery to these firms. In addition, some countries have also introduced new measures specifically orientated to such firms, introduced an element of discrimination in incentives in favour of small firms or redefined others to allow their inclusion via reduced eligibility thresholds or less onerous conditions. Other elements of the package of measures aimed at stimulating small business activity include the provision of information, advisory and consultancy facilities and the simplification of administrative procedures. These steps in incentives measures reflect a growing realisation of the important role of small business in terms of, for example, employment generation, innovation and entrepreneurship and their position in the overall industrial fabric of countries and regions.

Disincentives

In the OECD area, there has been a clear trend towards the removal or relaxation of disincentive measures. This can be seen as part and parcel of the broad trend towards liberalisation which also has been accompanied by deregulation, privatisation and generally greater freedom to the play of market forces in determining business decisions. As specifically concerns foreign direct investment, the declining use of measures with disincentive effects reflects the generally more positive perception of the contribution which such investment can make to the host economy. Not only do Member countries wish to attract foreign direct investment, but they are increasingly attempting to do so by a removal or reduction in measures which are felt to have a negative impact on investors' perception of the investment climate.

This broad trend is also paralleled in relation to TRIMs in the OECD area. In comparison to the situation at the beginning of the 80s, and while TRIMs were never all that widespread, there has been a significant reduction in their use which has generally occurred within the context of an overall liberalisation of measures affecting foreign investment. For example, in Canada, changes to the rules governing direct inward investment following the replacement of the Foreign Investment Review Board by Canada Investment, offered an opportunity to do away with local content and export requirements previously imposed. In Ireland, requirements for the local assembly of imported cars, introduced in 1968 to enable Irish industry to adapt, were dropped in 1985. In Portugal, local content and export requirements linked to the award of investment incentives have been abandoned so that assistance is no longer linked to any export or import restrictions. Nevertheless, a few countries still maintain TRIMs or measures which may have similar effects, generally geared to promoting equal opportunities for domestic enterprises in particular activities and their ability to compete for contracts. Most recently, and as indicated in chapter I, there has been growing concern with a number of developments, many related in one way or another to trade, which are seen as damaging to the investment climate as witnessed, for example, by the debate on local content or value added in determining the origin of products.

It is more difficult to say what is happening to performance requirements in the developing countries, in part due to lack of information and in part since there is evidence of moves in different countries in different directions. It nevertheless does seem that some countries have begun or are continuing to ease restrictions; newly industrialising economies such as Korea and Taiwan have, following the example of OECD countries, taken steps to reduce restrictions on international direct investment and bring their legislation more into line with that of the industrialised countries. In other countries where this trend is also apparent, it seems more directly linked to the fall in international direct investment in those countries and to debt difficulties and resulting problems, primarily in Latin America, as well as to a changing perception of the contribution of international direct investment to development.

However, other countries continue to apply measures which hinder investment. In Brazil, for instance, in spite of the deteriorating situation, restrictions on international investment have in general been maintained, or even increased, particularly in areas such as advanced technologies. In Mexico, even though foreign investors can acquire majority shareholdings, certain provisions are tending to strengthen local equity requirements. Several heavily indebted countries, which have admittedly eased controls on foreign investment, have taken steps to limit the outflow of capital, for example by restricting imports of equipment or repatriation of profits. Some of these measures are in principle temporary but, despite the easing of investment controls in the Andes Pact countries in general, some members of the Pact have tightened requirements imposed on foreign investors in sectors such as advanced technologies.

The above findings reveal diverse patterns in different countries. Some countries continue to ease their requirements; others, however, particularly if their economic situation continues to deteriorate, are liable to maintain or even step up restrictions to try and get the maximum benefit from investments, albeit at a time when international direct investment in the developing countries is hesitant.

2.   The effects of incentives and disincentives on direct international investment

The effects of investment incentives

Many of the broad conclusions of the 1983 study still remain valid today. This is hardly surprising as the major determinants of international direct investment are unchanged – market prospects, cost factors and corporate strategies still dominate these decisions. Similarly, and while there have been changes in incentives policies, these, as has been shown above, have not been of a nature to alter fundamentally their influence on international direct investment patterns. As such, investment incentives in general terms have only a limited and secondary effect on decisions to invest abroad and on the form of that investment. Incentives do of course influence cost considerations, particularly in periods of heightened cost consciousness. But often other costs, seen by business as more permanent or more geared to the fundamental soundness of the project are decisive. Indeed, from the perspective of the host country, investments that have been attracted because of incentives may not turn out to be sound in the longer term. Such situations are likely to arise the more investments are influenced by tax and other incentives vis-à-vis commercial considerations.

Incentives tend to exert a more significant influence at a later stage of the decision process, after the basic decisions concerning investment abroad (i.e., the decision to service a particular market or set of markets through establishment rather than through exports) have been taken. However, the general impact of international investment incentives on the broad directions of direct investment flows is also generally limited, although their effect here is likely to be stronger than that in relation to the volume or modalities of such flows. Incentives are likely to have a greater impact on the intra-regional location of investment, i.e., the choice of country (and sometimes the location within that country) within the world region relevant to the market the investment is intended to service. If, for example, a multinational enterprise is considering an investment in the European Community to serve that market, differences in the provision of incentives between different countries in the Community may strongly influence the actual country location chosen, along, obviously, with other factors such as the political and economic investment climate, availability of labour of the required characteristics, communications networks, etc.

An important question concerning this impact of investment incentives on location decisions is the extent to which broad similarities in the incentives systems in competing locations tend to cancel out their influence on this decision. It is often the case that a number of potential country locations within a given world region have relatively similar incentives systems. In these cases the investor may make his choice of location independent of incentives to the extent that a comparable level of assistance can be expected irrespective of the location chosen. However, this does not mean that any particular country would wish to reduce significantly its investment incentives and therefore that they are without any effect. As a result, significant reduction in incentives seems to require a multilateral approach. Furthermore, there are many important differences in the structure of incentive measures and these may be sufficient to avoid the type of stalemate situation suggested above.

Findings with respect to the impact of incentives on investment in the developing countries are quite similar to those for the OECD area. As a general rule, it seems that investment incentives of the type addressed in the Committee's study play a relatively limited role on investment decisions and that, in many cases, the main role of investment support is to offset the "tax" represented by performance requirements. However, one factor influencing the role played by investment incentives is whether the foreign investment is intended to replace imports by local production or is geared to production for export. In the former case, it is likely that the effect of incentives will be relatively limited. The existence of a specific and often protected market is often the major determinant of the investment, as market protection is a powerful incentive. In the second case, on the other hand, incentives are probably more important. Not only will investors often have the choice of several competing locations, but this type of investment, which has to be internationally competitive, is also more closely linked to cost considerations. However, the distinction between investment to serve the local market and investment for export is increasingly blurred today, as one set of countries, previously emphasising import substitution, is now pursuing export strategies to improve their debt situation, while another set is experiencing a development of local demand based on the income generated by successful export orientated strategies.

In comparison to the above generalised findings, it is worthwhile pointing out that a 1985 study by Guisinger et al on *Investment Incentives and Performance Requirements,* conducted for the International Finance Corporation, came up with results which, on the face of it are quite different. That study, which covered a period more or less comparable to that of the OECD's 1983 study, found that incentives often played a role significantly wider and stronger than that which emerges from the OECD and other studies. There are however, a number of important differences between the Guisinger and other studies, particularly in respect of methodology and definition which seem to explain this apparent discrepancy. For example, the Guisinger study uses a much broader definition of incentives which, in addition to fiscal, financial and non-financial investment incentives also includes commodity protection measures and "implicit" measures (such as the anticipated availability of government purchasing contracts). As has been noted above, trade protection measures can exert a very powerful influence on international direct investment and, indeed, Guisinger found that trade protection was in many cases a key factor in influencing investments, in particular, for a protected domestic or common market, with a lesser effect on investments geared to world markets. Other investment incentives, by comparison, appear to have little influence on decisions concerning investment in protected markets, but may play a stronger role for investments geared to serve a regional or world market. This is in line with the results of the OECD studies.

Turning to the more recent period, investment incentives do not seem to have had any greater impact on recent trends in international direct investment. The main factors determining these patterns continue to be economic conditions, policies of investing and host countries, the general climate for international investment, and technological development and the policies of multinational firms themselves. While there have been important changes over the period covered by this Review in the economic context for international direct investment, it does not appear that investment incentives have played any major new role in respect of the main patterns of change, including the overall expansion of outward investment, the substantial increase of international direct investment into the United States or the falling share of the developing countries in general or Latin America in particular. Within this broad picture, however, a number of developments in the context of international investments and incentives are worth mentioning.

The development of international direct investment reflects, among other things, the search for market outlets following technological innovations in fields such as electronics, computer services, telecommunications, robotics etc. These developments have and will have considerable repercussions on the structures and strategies of multinational enterprises and may, as discussed in Chapter VI, possibly lead to important changes in the location of certain investments. The nature of technological progress may perhaps strengthen the role of international investment incentives in some sectors, since the range of activities which can serve a global or regional market on a competitive basis from a small number of centres will tend to increase. Countries which were not hitherto rivals in attracting international direct investment may increasingly find themselves in competition with each other. Conclusions as to the effects of incentives on investment decisions may therefore have to be modified. Previously, incentives appeared to have a more important role in the choice between two countries in the same area but not between countries in different world regions. Technological innovations suggest that countries from totally different regions can now compete for a given investment (subject to them providing the investor with the necessary conditions, including an adequate skill base) and that incentives may have a stronger impact than in the past on the choice of location at the world level.

Major tax reforms in a number of OECD countries may also have implications for international direct investment. Countries which have substantially lowered the effective rates of tax on corporate profits may become more attractive locations for new investment. New firms may enter the market and existing firms expand their capacity. However, since taxation is not generally seen as a major influence on location decisions, it is unlikely that these reforms will have a major impact on direct investment patterns. Changes to tax systems may have some impact on the methods chosen to finance new investment (e.g. whether to arrange the financing via a third country) and the form that it takes (subsidiary versus a branch). Reforms which have lowered the rate of tax on profits may also encourage firms to repatriate profits, though this will depend in part on double taxation arrangements. At a more general level, the reduction in corporate tax rates, which has been widespread over the last three years, reduces the value of tax incentives and thereby reduces their influence on investment patterns.

Another policy development which, although not new, has gained greater importance in recent years is that of free trade zones (FTZs), through which important packages of incentives are increasingly offered. The benefits expected from FTZs in the OECD area have, however, often been disappointing. It is felt, for example, that their performance in attracting investment has been lackluster, with a stronger role being that of diverting investment into the zones from other parts of the country. Attractions with respect to cash flow and flexibility have sometimes been found to be of little relevance to some investors or they appear to offer few tangible benefits outside customs duty exemption for others. They may, however, be an attractive means of getting around import quotas by some reprocessing of goods to be sold on the domestic or common market and paying of the relevant duties.

Similarly, in developing countries, and while FTZs provide attractive sites and conditions for international direct investment, they have not proved a universal success story. In some countries, therefore, FTZs may be a necessary but by no means a sufficient requirement to attract international direct investment. Nevertheless, FTZs in Asia appear to have acted as a strong focal point for international direct investment, a considerable part of which was directed to the burgeoning zones and which was associated, in turn, with the strong export performance of many of the countries of the region.

In spite of these reservations, free zones are one of the few areas of investment incentives policy where competition among countries to attract direct investment is apparently becoming fiercer. Admittedly, results have perhaps not so far come up to expectations, but the fact that there are more and more of them shows the increasing interest in them, particularly in developing countries, following changing strategies of enterprises, trade conflicts and technological progress. The growth of and competition between FTZs has certain parallels with recent developments in financial centres, although here competition has so far not been related to incentives aspects but rather to the liberalisation of restrictive measures.

The effects of disincentives and trade-related investment measures

The effects of disincentives measures such as those referred to earlier in this chapter on investment flows may be wider than those of international investment incentives, as is clearly and obviously the case when investment in certain areas or activities is simply prohibited, or when conditions or requirements to be fulfilled in order for the investment to go ahead are so onerous that they are unacceptable to a wide range of enterprises regardless of other attractions or incentives. Even if the investment is permitted subject to preconditions or performance requirements, or when these conditions are attached to the award of incentives, such measures are generally perceived by business as indicative of the overall business climate in the country concerned and of its policy approach towards international direct investment. This is all the more so in the present period of heightened risk and uncertainty. In other words, the influence of the measures concerned on investment decisions may be considerably broader than the actual costs they would impose on investment projects.

Disincentive measures can obviously influence the location of international direct investment, and this influence may extend beyond locational choice within a given world region when, for example, the nature of preconditions or performance requirements in a country (or in the countries of a given world region) cause the investment not to go ahead at all or to be realised in a different world region. Disincentives may also affect other aspects of international direct investment decisions such as the modality and structure of the investment, for example, when local equity requirements interfere with the intention of some enterprises for full or majority ownership or when joint ventures are required by the host country.

Turning to the effects of individual measures, the investor, when faced with export requirements, may increase the size of his investment in view of the need to increase production capacity to supply markets not originally considered. Local content requirements may also lead to a change in the pattern of trade, which will however depend on the nature of the requirement imposed on the investor; if the requirement is expressed in terms of local production rather than purchases from local enterprises, the investor may decide to produce locally certain intermediate goods which he would otherwise have imported, so as to ensure quality and delivery. In addition, local content requirements may also affect investments as well as trade patterns in countries of origin or in third countries.

Technology transfer and local equity requirements may, for certain firms, have stronger disincentive effects than those associated with export or local content requirements. Clearly, if requirements are set too high they will be self defeating, but many enterprises do seem to be able, one way or another, to accommodate requirements, despite likely costs to the firm and the host country. By comparison, a firm with exclusive rights to a particular technology or on which its competitive advantage is founded will be extremely reluctant to transfer it, particularly where intellectual property rights are poorly protected or when the transfer is not justified by economies of scale, market prospects or the state of competition. Acceptance of such a constraint may cause changes to production levels, the range of products and prices and this may impair the overall viability of the investment. Local equity requirements may quite simply deter investors for whom retention of ownership and control is part of their business philosophy. Where they do not deter the investor, they may, if the risks involved are felt to be excessive or the quality of proposed local associates inadequate, cause them to reconsider the nature of the project and to reduce it to the minimum compatible with the requirements of the host country. More generally, the accommodation of performance requirements by firms results in increased costs, not only to the enterprise itself but also to the host country and the consumer.

The effects of these measures can differ depending on the industries affected. It seems that the motor vehicle industry for example has been a general target for performance requirements and these companies have, as a result often had to undertake further defensive investment in order to preserve access to the domestic market or to maintain market shares previously gained by exports. The food industry seems much more affected by restrictions on the repatriation of profits and by the payment of special charges, price controls or employment requirements. Similarly, export requirements are felt to be a severe constraint by these industries and they have led to the abandonment of certain projects. In information technology, local equity and technology transfer requirements are the ones which business view as least acceptable.

The essential point to be emphasised is that beyond their economic impact per se or the market correction argument, preconditions and performance requirements are seen by investors as disincentives and as indicative of the investment climate in the host country, including the treatment of private investment in general and international direct investment in particular. This basic perception does not appear to be attenuated much by the fact that the countries using preconditions and performance requirements also often offer investment incentives, which are frequently seen by business as necessary to offset the additional costs resulting from performance requirements.

Effects of combined incentive and disincentive measures

Disincentives and trade-related investment measures often exist in combination with incentives in many countries, particularly developing countries. In fact, and taking a wider view of incentives, the situation in some developing countries is one where trade protection, performance requirements and investment incentives are frequently found together. This raises the question of why such countries operate a package of measures containing incentives and disincentives rather than having neither of these types of measures, when a main function of incentives, at least as seen by business and particularly in relation to the developing countries, is to offset the additional costs resulting from performance requirements.

At the aggregate level, the principal factors influencing the location of international direct investment are market prospects and cost factors together with the nature, stability and transparency of investment conditions, with the role played by investment incentives and disincentives being generally of a secondary nature. However, once a broader view is taken of incentives, particularly when trade protection measures are included, a much more significant influence can be ascribed to incentives, as these types of measures are closely associated with market attraction and prospects. The strength of this attraction may be such that it permits or facilitates the use of performance requirements, in which case the latter cannot be seen as a primary determinant of location. However, it has also been noted that performance requirements may have an independent locational impact, as for example, when they result in additional, defensive investments. The main role ascribed in the above argument for investment incentives is therefore that of offsetting the costs resulting from performance requirements.

Of course, particular types of performance requirements or the levels at which they are set may be regarded by business as unacceptable, or the level of awards in investment incentive schemes may be seen as insufficient compensation, in which case the investment may be abandoned, relocated or altered in some other manner.

Even if performance requirements and incentives cancel each other out at the enterprise level such that the investment goes ahead (just as similar investment incentive provisions between different countries may neutralise their effect on influencing the choice of location between the countries concerned) this is not without a general loss to economic efficiency and a cost to the taxpayer who must pay for the incentives. In addition, it is often likely that the characteristics of that investment (e.g. in respect of size, organisational structure, purchasing and trading patterns) are different from those which would have arisen from a situation of no incentives and no requirements.

Although incentives and disincentives may, in some sense or another, cancel each other out, the assessment by business of the impact of these measures is not simply one of finding equivalent values for different measures and calculating some net financial effect. As noted above, incentives and disincentives may be perceived very differently by business; it is one thing to assist investors to do what they would like to and an entirely different matter to restrict or prohibit it, or to impose requirements on how it should be carried out.

As seen from the above discussion, disincentives, in comparison to investment incentives, are likely to have a wider impact on international direct investment decisions;

they are more closely associated with investors' perception of the business climate, their impacts on investment may be more diverse and they can influence more components of the overall international direct investment decision (e.g., the decision to undertake international direct investment over exports, the form and other characteristics of the investment and its timing) in addition to its location. Furthermore, these measures, and this is also true for investment incentives, may still have important effects on trade flows or on resource allocation even in the absence of effects on investment (while the existence of investment effects obviously results in trade effects through import substitution or export generation). Indeed the measures concerned would generally affect the costs or benefits attached to a particular project, even though they may not be sufficient to modify the investment aspects of the project (size, timing, location, etc.). Trade effects of the measures concerned are thus, in general, to be seen as more prevalent than investment effects.

The Committee's analysis of trends and effects of international investment incentives and disincentives has shown that while considerable progress has been made in some areas, there is a growing need to improve international co-operation in this area. In respect of incentives, there has been a noticeable rationalisation and reorientation of measures in OECD countries, in part geared to avoiding or reducing distortive effects on investment, but Member countries still spent large amounts of public money on these measures. While attention has increasingly turned to removing or relaxing disincentives to attract international direct investment, it is still the case that, if countries would wish to achieve substantial reductions in expenditure on investment without compromising their ability to attract direct investment, multilateral co-operation will be essential.

In respect of disincentives, there has been considerable progress in OECD countries with their removal, which is part of the broader move towards less intervention and greater recourse to market forces. The situation in developing countries as concerns disincentives is much less clear and certainly more diverse. With a pronounced deceleration of international direct investment in developing countries there does appear to be a broad change in the appreciation of developing countries about the role of international direct investment and its contribution to development. Similarly, there are signs of a greater appreciation that the negative effects of disincentives are even stronger in periods of slow growth and high uncertainty. In some developing countries, this has been translated into the removal or relaxation of disincentives with a view to attracting international direct investment, but in other cases it is also apparent that disincentive measures have been maintained, increased or introduced, in a more defensive approach to forestall, for example, further capital outflows or ensure what benefit they can from existing investment.

If growth in the developing countries begins to pick up, the question will arise as to whether certain relaxations in disincentives will be maintained or whether there will be a return to policy approaches of the 70s. It is therefore very opportune that the Uruguay Round of GATT negotiations is addressing investment measures with trade restrictive or distorting effects. Progress in the Uruguay Round would make a significant contribution to the climate for international investment on two related fronts – bringing TRIMs, which have become a serious concern on a number of fronts, under multilateral discipline, while progress more generally on trade measures will contribute to a reduction in trade frictions which have overlapped into the international investment area and given rise to, or at least hindered the removal, of certain trade related disincentives to international investment.

Chapter VI

INTERNATIONAL DIRECT INVESTMENT
IN NON-MEMBER COUNTRIES

The 1980s has been a period of growing integration of the world economy and globalisation of business strategies. At the same time, serious problems related to the lack of sustained growth and debt problems in many non-Member countries have persisted or emerged. International direct investment has a distinct and important contribution to make, yet the ability of many non-member countries in some areas to attract this investment slumped quite drastically at the beginning of the 80s, at a time when it was most needed, and it is only now showing signs of recovering to previous levels.

Not surprisingly, foreign direct investment tends to flow to countries offering economic and political stability, attractive growth prospects and a clear investment regime setting the conditions within which foreign investors will operate. In recent years, an increasing number of non-Member governments have recognised the need to improve the climate for private investment in their countries if they are to be more attractive to foreign investors and have taken steps to adjust their policies in this direction. Concern over national sovereignty has been giving way to more pragmatic approaches designed to encourage capital and know-how needed for economic growth and development. These changes are as yet far from universal, but the trend is clear and the need to compete for scarce investment capital may well sustain the movement.

The work of the Committee has concentrated on better understanding the situation in non-Member countries through, for example, its assessment of trends in international direct investment and analysis of the role played by the debt situation, technological developments and the policy environment. It has also been examining ways and means to increase the flow of international direct investment and its contribution to development, through Round Tables and Seminars on foreign direct investment, and its support for internationally agreed rules of the game. The Committee believes that its efforts in these areas have contributed to the more positive view that is already emerging in non-Member countries of the contribution that international direct investment can make to their economic development. More recently the Committee has begun to play an active role in the Organisation's growing activities in relation to Central and Eastern Europe, the Dynamic Asian Economies and Latin America.

1. Trends in international direct investment in non-Member countries

In sharp contrast to the OECD area where most countries experienced rapid growth in FDI flows from abroad, few non-Member countries participated in the boom in foreign direct investment in the 1980s (see Table 4). Except for the DAEs and the offshore banking centres in Latin America, non-Member countries experienced no increase in annual FDI inflows over the decade whereas, over the period 1975-79 non-Member countries as a whole were able to attract an increasing share of foreign direct investment. The share of FDI in total private flows to non-Member countries rose from below 20 per cent at the beginning of the decade to around 60 per cent on average for the years 1987 to 1989, but this was mainly due to a drying up of bank lending (which averaged $7 billion per annum for 1986 to 1989, in comparison to the 1981 high of $52 billion).

There are very marked differences in economic performance among the different geographical regions and these are reflected in the flows of foreign direct investment. There has been a geographic redistribution of international direct investment flows to the non-Member countries, with flows to Asia expanding at the expense of Latin America and Africa and, within regions, some countries are more favoured than others. Flows to central and eastern European economies have been negligible to date. Across a broad geographical front, low growth, high debt and inappropriate policies both at the macro and micro level caused a major deterioration in the attractiveness of countries to foreign investors, many of whom have looked increasingly to the OECD area and to other countries where medium and longer term growth prospects are more favourable. There has also been a shift in FDI away from investment in raw material and intensive labour production in which developing countries have a comparative advantage to more high technology-oriented manufacturing and service industries.

The outlook for the period ahead is perhaps more promising. Improved economic management and structural reforms have resulted in more outward-looking policies, and a more welcoming attitude towards foreign investment can only improve the chances of attracting much needed capital and expertise to exploit the considerable investment opportunities in non-Member countries. If confidence in the maintenance of sound policies can be established and sustained, investment flows to less developed countries can be expected to expand again.

Asia

Asia's share of international direct investment flows has increased from 26 per cent in 1976-83 to 32 per cent in 1984-89; since 1987, there has been a jump in international direct investment to the DAEs and more recently in the ASEAN countries[1], most of this expansion being attributable to higher Japanese investment but also, increasingly, to the United States and some European countries. Foreign direct investment flows to Asia are concentrated in a small number of economies: Hong Kong, Indonesia, Malaysia, Korea, Singapore, Taiwan and Thailand. Inflows to these economies tripled (to $23 billion) over the decade and their share of Asian inflows jumped from 35 per cent to 72 per cent between 1981 and 1989. While all of the DAEs have shared in this expansion, it can be noted that, since 1988, flows to Korea and Hong Kong have taken a downward turn due, respectively, to the effects of higher unit labour costs and future political uncertainties, but growth remained high in Malaysia, Philippines, Indonesia and Thailand. Reasons for the rapid growth of FDI to the DAEs may be found in the success of domestic economic policies and the growth of the region's economy.

The sectoral composition of inward investment in Asia has also been changing, indicating industrial restructuring similar to that experienced by Japan in the 70s. The weight of the non-manufacturing sector is tending to increase, while the manufacturing sector is undergoing a transformation that will probably strengthen advanced technology sectors such as information technology, electronics and biotechnology. In Korea, for example, foreign investment is particularly welcome in the information technology, electronics and plastics sectors, insofar as it is accompanied by the transfer of advanced technology, while US firms have expanded high value-added production and R&D activities in Singapore. In the DAEs, FDI has declined in labour intensive industries, but has risen in technology intensive and services sectors. The rapid growth of FDI in the region has created a growing demand for technicians, managers and skilled labour which has caused wages to soar.

Among non-Member countries, China lies apart; since opening its economy to foreign investment, China has become a host country to foreign investment, receiving nearly 6 per cent of total foreign investment in developing countries between 1980 and 1985. The number of investments authorised in 1985 was particularly high, related to the decision to open up several coastal towns and Special Economic Zones to private investment. Since then, the number of authorisations has tended to fall, awaiting a change in policy orientation from investments in hotels and service activities to industrial and capital intensive activities. Foreign investment rose sharply in China in 1988 and through the first half of 1989, but fell off following the events of June 1989 and the subsequent economic retrenchment. Major setbacks in the political liberalisation process have slowed down the momentum towards economic reform and momentarily limited inward FDI; nevertheless, considering that a more closed attitude to foreign direct investment would deprive the country of its associated benefits, and make it more difficult to fulfil its development goals, since late 1990 China has again welcomed foreign investors.

Latin America

In comparison, over the same period of time, the ten largest Latin America countries have received net flows of FDI, relative to GDP, of only half those registered by Asian countries. This disappointing performance was frequently the result of policies designed to limit and regulate investment, which in many cases fostered inefficient industries. Moreover the instability of economic policies contributed to raising risks and limiting returns on investment. This is related to the fact that many of the countries in Latin America have been confronted, to a much greater extent than the other non-Member countries, with the problem of servicing and rescheduling external debt. External imbalances, depressed domestic demand and swings in exchange rates, together with high inflation and political tensions, have created a climate that is not conducive to international direct investment. These factors, coupled with restrictions on imports and the repatriation of capital, have contributed to the decline in international direct investment in the area until 1987. Inward investment to most of these countries has been flat or in decline over the first half of the 1980s and did not catch up with the 1981 peak of $17 billion until after 1986. At $30 billion in 1989, flows to Latin American countries accounted for 50 per cent of direct investment flows to non-Member countries, but these figures are heavily influenced by investment in offshore banking centres (the Bahamas,

Bermuda, the Cayman Islands, the Netherlands Antilles and Panama) and by investment in countries offering flags of convenience. These countries increased their share of Latin American inflows from 16 per cent in 1983 to 56 per cent by 1989.

There has been little investment in new plant and equipment, most of the investment being made to replace or to modernise existing operations, except in Colombia where there has been major investment in the mining sector. The survival of manufacturing industries will depend on their ability to become competitive vis-à-vis the industrialised countries and the Dynamic Asian Economies. US companies have traditionally been the leading investors in Latin America, but their investment in the region has been falling off, while there has been a relative increase in that by Japanese, British and German firms. The scientific and technological infrastructure that Latin America needs in order to expand is still weak; adjustments and innovations are required to achieve a capital-labour-new technology mix better adapted to the present competitive situation.

Recent years have witnessed the beginning of a change in economic policy thinking in certain countries in Latin America, geared to restoring credibility and creditworthiness. There is growing recognition of the need for outward looking and liberal economic, trade and investment policies if these countries are to participate fully in a technology-based globalising world economy. Mexico provides a good example of how sound macroeconomic policies and structural reforms provide the basis for a prudent recovery, which has also been associated with tripling of foreign direct investment over the period 1986-89 (to $1.5 billion) and a return of flight capital.

Africa

The situation in Africa is disquieting. Even in the late 1970s, Africa received only 10 per cent of investment flows to developing countries and since then the situation has further deteriorated. Non-market orientated economic policies and political instability, together with poor infrastructure, small local markets, the absence of a trained labour force, flat international demand for raw materials and the increase in the region's external debt continue to make large parts of Africa unattractive to foreign investors.

Nevertheless, more African governments are taking a more positive attitude towards FDI and several African countries have begun vigorously looking for FDI to relaunch their economies. Nigeria, Kenya and Zimbabwe have improved the regulatory framework for FDI and have been privatising some state-owned enterprises. For all but a few African countries (Liberia, Nigeria, Zimbabwe), however, there has been little new FDI, and some companies have disinvested.

Central and Eastern Europe

FDI in Central and Eastern Europe has been relatively unimportant in respect of total outward investment from the OECD area. The main form of foreign involvement in the region was in joint ventures. It is estimated that by 1989, the number of joint ventures registered in the Czech and Slovak Federal Republic (CSFR), Hungary, Poland and the Soviet Union was around 4 000 in total, representing a foreign capital participation of around $2 billion; 1989 had witnessed a major jump in joint venture activity, with over 1 000 approvals. Half of these were in the Soviet Union, with Hungary and then Poland accounting for most of the rest; with the main sectors of activity being manufacturing, financial services and hotels and restaurants.

Thus far, the overall result with joint ventures have been disappointing. Foreign interests in the countries of the region have not matched the expectations of the host countries as most of the investments expected through negotiations did not materialise or only on a very small scale. The amount of foreign capital actually committed is often in the range of 10 to 20 per cent of total planned expenditure. Free trade zones are now being set up or planned, notably in Poland, Hungary and USSR, as a means of attracting foreign investment to produce goods and services for both export and the local market.

The development of the services sector, particularly banking and financial services, telecommunications, information technology and transport, has a crucial role to play in these economies. The present situation is one of under-investment, production and service facilities being old and outmoded, due to past reluctance to invest in civil equipment and infrastructure; thus the civilian sector so far has not benefited much from the advances in new technologies. At present, the services sector represents a bottleneck to the process of structural adjustment. The major avenues to develop the services sector are privatisation and FDI, the latter particularly in the areas of financial services, telecommunications, business services and transportation. In most of these countries special plans have been adopted for the development and modernisation of the telecommunication network with the assistance of international firms and organisations.

2. The impact of external debt on international direct investment in non-Member countries

The particularly favourable growth period for non-Member countries as a whole ended with the world recession at the beginning of the 1980s. This had profound consequences for a number of countries which had built up their external debt position to untenable levels, partly to finance ambitious industrial projects in line with the unbundling of international direct investment packages and partly to finance natural resource investments that often yielded lower-than-anticipated returns. The resultant debt burden and required policy adjustments meant that many non-Member countries were not in a position to benefit from the 1980s recovery in the OECD area. Indeed, many of the initial policies adopted in response to debt and recession (with respect to savings, investment, the public sector, fiscal, monetary, etc.) were poorly thought-out or implemented, with counterproductive results. High levels of external indebtedness have underlined the need to encourage as much capital inflow as possible and, in particular, stable flows of productive equity funds. At the same time, international bank lending, whose volume had come to exceed that of direct investment to non-Member countries, has now become much more scarce, as the banking sector has moved to limit its developing country exposure.

Since the debt crisis, indebted countries' perception of international direct investment has been changing with greater emphasis given to its positive attributes, in particular that it is a non-debt creating capital flow and that it contributes to longer term development and structural adjustment. Recently, new forms of financing and techniques have emerged in highly indebted countries to enhance direct investment and other financial flows. The contribution of international direct investment to resolving the debt situation in non-Member countries should not be seen solely in terms of the volume of capital inflows in relation to debt servicing burdens and the fact that, unlike debt finance, subsequent repayments are closely tied to the profitability of the investment. Direct investment has other important attributes, including managerial and marketing techniques, technology transfer and other aspects of the international direct investment package which contribute to the ability of developing countries to undertake structural adjustments. In fact, it is the greater recognition of these attributes and the contribution they can make to adjustment which is behind much of the change in attitudes to international direct investment that has been occurring.

Efforts to promote international direct investment represents only one of the approaches undertaken to contribute to a reduction of the debt burden, and its role has therefore to be seen together with other arrangements such as debt rescheduling or debt-equity conversion schemes. An increase in international direct investment flows is particularly attractive to the heavily-indebted countries, on account of the long-term effects on their productive potential, industrial restructuring and balance of payments. As the debt situation evolves, higher inflows of direct investment would be a useful complement to the debt and debt service reduction strategies along the lines proposed in the Brady initiative.

Debt conversion schemes, which were specially designed for heavily-indebted countries, have made it possible to increase international direct investment to these countries while at the same time reducing their outstanding external debt. Banks, investors and indebted countries all stand to gain from debt-equity conversion schemes. They allow banks to rationalise their holdings and to cut their losses, even when the discount attains 20 and even 60 per cent of the real value of their claims. For the investor who purchases the debt, they represent an opportunity to increase an existing interest in local industries or to fund new projects on more advantageous terms. They allow the indebted countries to replace costly debt servicing by foreign equity holdings; the essential aim is to promote additional investment in these countries, this is possible only if the capital stemming from the debt conversion is not in lieu of foreign funds that have already been earmarked for investment projects and if the project would not have been implemented without the injection of foreign funds.

To date, several heavily-indebted countries (Argentina, Brazil, Chile, Costa Rica, Ecuador, Mexico, the Philippines and Venezuela) have taken advantage of the possibilities offered by these schemes. The external debt/GNP ratio of these countries rose from slightly over 30 per cent in 1982 to 55 per cent in 1987. These countries have been increasingly obliged, therefore, to seek fresh public or private capital overseas, and to reduce their external debt by recourse to market-based arrangements. New techniques offering "à la carte" participation have made it easier for commercial banks to take part in agreements to reschedule debt and to provide new funds, and at the same time have reduced these countries' debt. Since 1985, the implementation of debt-equity conversion programmes has accelerated generating new international direct investment flows to the indebted countries.

By end-1987, total debt conversion amounted to some $7 billion, which may not seem much compared with the debt of the five most heavily-indebted countries ($212 billion) but which, all things considered, is fairly substantial when compared with the volume of international direct investment in the same countries during the first half of the 1980s. Moreover, debt equity swaps helped to revive FDI to Latin America in the late 1980s, being especially important in Chile, Brazil and Mexico. Programmes in Latin America accounted for $4.3 billion in 1988, but only $1.3 billion in 1989, owing to the interruption of swaps in Mexico, Brazil, and political instability in Colombia. Swaps programmes resumed in 1990 to reach $4 billion, the bulk going to manufacturing, partly because of restrictions on investment in mining, petroleum, and in the financial sector and other services. New programmes in Argentina, Mexico and Brazil focus on the financing of the sale of state enterprises and other assets of the public sector (e.g. telephone companies and airlines).

The use of swaps in the privatisation of state owned companies is a positive development, the local currency disbursements being financed by the issuance of shares in the privatised companies to foreign investors. It facilitates ownership and control of inefficient state owned companies by private companies with access to better and more up to date technology, production, management and marketing systems. One particular impediment to debt-equity conversion is the scarcity of investment opportunities relative to the size of the debt. Some sectors, particularly those that host countries regard as strategic, remain closed to inward investment. In effect, indebted countries fear that foreign investment in these sectors will impair their national sovereignty and result in their industries coming completely under foreign control. Problems of this nature might be alleviated by allowing residents as well as non-residents to benefit from the opportunities opened up by debt conversion, and by considering alternative schemes, for example involving co-ownership with local institutions, which could be proposed to foreign investors.

It can also assist in the repatriation of flight capital enabling domestic investors to acquire funds at more advantageous rates through the discount on the value of developing countries' debt. On the other hand, it may lead to ''round-tripping'' i.e. capital that would otherwise have remained within the country is transferred abroad and then repatriated, allowing a capital gain to be made on the debt-equity swap, and contributing to inflationary pressures.

Generally speaking, conversion schemes can avoid inflationary effects if properly structured and implemented, with accompanying measures at the macroeconomic level such as those to promote higher domestic saving. However, there may be an inflationary risk if a country implements a programme under which the loan is swapped for local currency that is used to finance consumer expenditure or activities that involve capital flight more or less directly.

3. Technological innovation and international direct investment

Technological advances, too, have had important repercussions for international direct investment in the non-Member countries. Major developments such as those in the fields of robotics and new materials may reduce the comparative advantage of these countries in areas where labour costs and raw materials used to play a major role, while advances in other areas such as telecommunications might facilitate investment in non-Member countries. In particular, such developments are having wide-ranging implications for production and business organisation. If some of the non-Member countries were to become cut off from the new technological era due to an insufficient capacity to absorb and use this technology, this would make them even less prepared for the eventual resumption of growth and the consequences of newer technologies on the horizon.

These technological innovations may cause certain locational advantages to shift back to the most industrialised economies, since many of the innovations render offshore production based on previous technology less competitive or even obsolete. Many of these innovations, such as robotics, are labour-saving and thus tend to reduce the attractiveness of investment in low-labour cost countries. On the other hand, those in the computer and telecommunications field could encourage or facilitate decentralisation of production and thereby increase the chances of the most dynamic countries. For example, flexible manufacturing systems make short production runs profitable, and decentralised communications systems eliminate the need for integrating decision centres and production sites.

It is therefore not easy to predict how important and long-lasting the effects of these new technologies will be on developing countries' competitiveness and their ability to attract international direct investment. Their ability to assimilate new technologies will be determined by a set of factors related to local conditions, such as the availability of a well-trained labour force and high-grade infrastructure. There is also a risk, for at least some countries, of an eventual de-coupling of their industrial activities from those of more industrialised countries, if they are unable to attract the new technologies, which could result in them being left permanently behind and unable to take advantage of the resumption of economic growth.

In the present situation, where the new technologies and related know-how represent a major competitive asset for the firms concerned, the latter have no desire to lose any advantage as a result of practices that are gaining ground due to the lack of protection of industrial property. Counterfeiting and piracy are problems for traditional technologies as well as for new ones, but they are particularly serious for the latter, since firms depend crucially on their technological edge. The broad issue of protecting intellectual property extends far beyond that of counterfeiting and piracy, since inadequate protection of patent-holders can have the same damaging effects even without actual counterfeiting. It also goes beyond the area of international direct investment, encompassing other forms of international economic relations such as trade. It may also have a significant impact on the flow of direct investment particularly to the Dynamic Asian Economies and some Latin America countries. Unless satisfactory solutions can be found, many enterprises are likely to target their investment efforts to an even greater extent on developed countries rather than jeopardise their technological lead. It is therefore essential that there is greater recognition of the possible effects on international direct investment patterns resulting from the poor protection of industrial property rights and that steps are taken to achieve an effective solution to this problem. This is an area where in the past there have been clear conflicts between the interests of some non-Member countries and some multinational enterprises and where the Uruguay Round negotiations on this subject could make a major contribution if significant progress is achieved.

4. Policies of non-Member countries towards direct investment

In contrast with OECD Member countries, there is not such a general acceptance in non-Member countries of the advantages of liberal international direct investment policies. Over the past forty years, non-Member countries' attitudes towards international direct investment have varied widely, ranging from the very liberal to the highly restrictive. During this period there have been two opposing conceptions of international direct investment. Policy-makers in a few countries have always been convinced of the benefits of foreign direct investment; for them, such investment constitutes a tightly bound package of capital inflows, of technologies that are often new to the host country, and of managerial and marketing services that are locally in short supply. Furthermore, the experience with technologies and services capabilities of the foreign enterprise gained by local firms and their suppliers and clients on the spot is likely to be transmitted to some extent to the rest of the economy.

Non-Member countries' critics of foreign direct investment have, on the contrary, stressed that a significant proportion of capital inflows is likely to be spent on imported equipment or other inputs, and that the transfer of profits abroad tends to be excessive. In their view, multinational enterprises have a bias for imported rather than local supplies, while the experience gained with new technologies is minor, or inaccessible to local firms because of the gap between imported technologies and those that can develop locally on any significant scale. As a consequence of these negative perceptions, the attitude towards international direct investment has been highly restrictive in many non-Member countries which have implemented a range of controls and conditions with a view to increasing developmental benefits derived from direct investment.

While many non-Member countries often continue to maintain major restrictions on international direct investment, their policy approach is tending to become less restrictive. The relaxations which have taken place in some countries and for certain activities suggest that these countries are attempting to strike a new balance between economic and political pressures in their policies in order to attract more investment. The counter-productive results of many non-Member countries' previous domestic policies have clearly influenced these changes which should lead, through the implementation of successful structural adjustment programmes, to an improvement in the climate for private business in general, a feature considered by multinational enterprises as a prerequisite for investment. In fact, investors have sometimes reported that their problems with doing business in some non-Member countries stem as much from general attitudes to private investment and market forces per se as from the discriminatory treatment of foreign owned companies. The change in attitude towards foreign investment itself, which is increasingly seen as making a positive contribution in the context of more market-oriented domestic policies is also encouraging. More and more non-Member countries – even those in which inward direct investment was formerly not allowed, or for all practical purposes, impossible – now actively seek to attract foreign investors and many have relaxed their foreign investments regimes. Some still retain enabling interventionist legislation, but grant more and more authorisations in an increasing number of sectors, and forego some conditions that they tended to enforce strictly in the past.

In some cases the liberalisation of these economies has resulted from increasing recognition of the contribution of international direct investment to development; in other cases, it is more a response to an unfavourable economic environment. For example, given the deterioration in their balance of payments as a result of the fall in commodity prices and the worsening of their external debt, some Asian countries (Korea, Malaysia and Thailand) modified their attitude and, to varying degrees, their laws and regulations concerning foreign direct investment, and have followed long-established free-market economies like Hong Kong, Singapore and Taiwan in opening up their economies to foreign capital. The emphasis has been put on simplifying the approval procedures for foreign investment (India, Indonesia and the Philippines) and on changing the laws and regulations concerning the level of foreign participation in domestic firms and take-overs by foreign firms (Indonesia and Malaysia). Other countries have altered the conditions of access to sectors that were previously closed to foreign investment.

Major changes in legislation and policies have also taken place in Latin America. Restrictions on foreign ownership and management control have been lifted over the period in many of the countries of the region; for example, local participation requirements in certain sectors have been eased considerably in many countries. Progress in removing restrictions on remittances of profits and capital has been somewhat slower, but in the last two years there has been a marked acceleration in the pace of reform of regulations and legislation governing foreign direct investment. Argentina, Costa Rica, Mexico and Venezuela introduced major changes in foreign direct investment codes in 1989 and 1990, liberalising the regimes for the operation of foreign firms. Chile already had an open regime concerning foreign direct investment.

Progress remains to be made in a number of areas, even in countries with liberal investment regime. Investment in the financial sector is restricted, legal barriers to foreign direct investment in commercial banking and other financial institutions exist in many countries. In others, new investments in commercial banking are barred. Restrictions on imports of inputs or local content requirements in certain industries also present difficulties to prospective investors. New restrictions have been introduced in some sectors, particularly those involving new technology (Brazil, Mexico); likewise, technology transfers and technology imports by the public sector have come under increasingly tight control. However, it seems clear that the liberalisation of international direct investment in some Latin American countries is illustrative of a generally more favourable attitude.

In Central and Eastern Europe, by the end of the 1980s, almost all the countries of the region had started to liberalise their investment regimes, with equity participation of foreign-controlled enterprises, particularly through joint ventures in order to increase their attractiveness to foreign investors. Apart from joint ventures, other quasi-investment arrangements include buy-back operations, co-production agreements and leasing arrangements. In almost all countries legislation has been revised and improved, and since 1989 majority foreign ownership is permitted in all of the countries, with full foreign ownership being permitted in Hungary, Poland and the Czech and Slovak Federal Republic. Authorisation and registration procedures have been simplified, and there has been a general opening up of the areas and activities where foreign involvement is permitted unless not compatible with national security interests, although preference may still be given to particular sectors or activities. In the USSR too, there have been important developments, although the liberalisation trends have been more cautious in comparison to countries such as Hungary and Poland.

It is still too early to indicate the likely effects on inward direct investment of the changes in legislation mentioned above, but these changes clearly go in the direction of providing a legal framework more attractive to foreign investors. Investors still face considerable uncertainties as to the conditions which will govern their operations in many of these countries. Traditional problems of doing business in central and eastern European countries (such as non-convertibility of currencies, repatriation restrictions, inadequate infrastructure, the economic and financial situation of the host country and the more general and bureaucratic problems associated with conducting business) will have to be overcome.

In Africa, several countries have also implemented investment codes to encourage international direct investment (Ivory Coast, Ghana, Zambia, Cameroon, Burkina Faso). Broadly speaking, the aim of these codes is to abolish local participation requirements and to restrict the number of sectors reserved to domestic investors. Likewise, a number of countries (such as Angola, Burundi, Somalia and Zimbabwe) have taken steps to abolish restrictions on the repatriation of profits.

Among non-Member countries there has been considerable movement in their approaches towards foreign direct investment and in the direction of greater openness and liberalisation through privatisation. Privatisation programmes have been implemented in countries such as Argentina, Chile, Malaysia, Pakistan, the Philippines, Nigeria and Senegal, whose public sectors were often perceived as having grown too large and inefficient. Such programmes can open up a number of sectors to international direct investment that were formerly closed; they are often complementary to debt conversion policies. Although privatisation programmes have been implemented in many countries and sectors, sometimes they have proceeded at a fairly slow pace, either because the local financial markets did not have the capacity to handle them, or because the assets proposed offered a low return.

Privatisation has now become an important element in the restructuring policies of the countries of Central and Eastern Europe. Foreign capital is essential to the privatisation process given the paucity of private domestic capital and the lack of domestic capital market. While the overall amount of capital injection might be relatively small in relation to local financial needs, FDI is expected to play an important catalytic role in attracting other funds. Similarly, other components of the investment package, as noted above, are central to the transition of these economies. In that respect, Poland aims at transferring the financial burden of state owned enterprises from the State to the private sector by converting debt into equity. In addition, the new law on foreign investment in Yugoslavia permits the financing of such investments through the purchase of local currency at a discount on the secondary market.

5.   OECD Member countries' policies towards direct investment in non-Member countries

In the period covered by this Review there have also been important developments in the policies and approaches of Member countries and of international organisations, all geared to improving the flow of international direct investment to non-Member countries. For example, technical assistance has developed considerably in the areas of technology transfer and assimilation, vocational training and investment policy and development planning. Within the framework of the OECD's Development Assistance Committee, Member countries have stressed the need to co-ordinate closely official development assistance (ODA) and private sector development, including private investment. The arguments in favour of such co-ordination show that technical assistance and ODA can be used as a catalyst to private sector development, including international direct investment. However, care has to be taken that direct support for private investment via ODA avoids creating distortions in capital flows and interfering with the development of market forces to be promoted. It has also been claimed that the technology transfers associated with ODA are of a different type from those under private investment as well as being of lower quality.

Another relevant development over the last years is that the international financial institutions have sought to promote the growth of financial markets in non-Member countries with a view to encouraging and harnessing national savings. By 1988, there were already ten investment funds for the heavily-indebted countries in operation.

Multilateral and bilateral aid agencies provide developing countries with financial aid on concessional terms for infrastructure, teaching and training, thereby laying the foundations for a build-up of the private sector in these countries while at the same time encouraging international direct investment. The assistance provided by some institutions to domestic banks also serves to finance the projects of small domestic enterprises. In recent years these institutions have diversified their activities in order to meet the needs of foreign and domestic investors and the financing requirements arising from structural adjustment policies.

In the area of international co-operation, April 1988 saw the effective start-up of the Multilateral Investment Guarantee Agency (MIGA). This Agency hopes to make an important contribution to the growth of international direct investment in developing countries through its insurance mechanisms. By providing guarantees, co-insuring or reinsuring non-commercial risks (e.g. transfer, expropriation, non-compliance with contracts, armed conflict or social unrest), and by offering a wide range of services to facilitate investment, particularly technical assistance and policy advice, the MIGA intends to reduce considerably investors' risk exposure. It is likely to have an impact on a wide range of foreign investors, and not just those who merely want insurance. Recent steps such as the guaranteed recovery of investment schemes set up by the International Finance Corporation (IFC) and the guarantee provided by the Overseas Private Investment Corporation (OPIC) to investment fund investors are further examples of the diversification of the types of guarantee now available.

At the bilateral level, there has been a very marked expansion in the use of bilateral investment agreements, such that over 270 agreements have been concluded between Member and non-Member countries by the end of 1988. This expansion is a further sign of the growing interrelationships and co-operation between home and host countries in the area of international direct investment. Indeed, many countries now operate an investment guarantee scheme only if a bilateral agreement exists. These schemes, which are complemented by MIGA, aim to provide better protection for investors and to improve the host country's international image as an investment location.

The Committee is well aware that the promotion of international direct investment in non-Member countries is a complicated task that requires a combined effort on the part of all the parties concerned – private firms, international organisations, host and home country governments. Noting that an increasing number of non-Member countries were introducing more favourable foreign investment regimes and lowering existing barriers, and in order to encourage international direct investment, the Committee has organised two Round Tables with the objectives of permitting open and frank exchanges of views between these parties and of seeking pragmatic ways and means to promote international direct investment in non-Member countries.

The first Round Table on "Foreign Direct Investment and Development" was jointly organised in 1986 in West Berlin by the Committee and the Development Policy Forum of the German Foundation for International Development. This Round Table highlighted the changes in the conditions for investment in non-Member countries, especially factors such as host countries' policies towards foreign investors and the change of attitude towards international direct investment and the role that it can play in development. Particular note was taken of the importance attached by many non-Member countries to the need to reduce the overall role of the State and to strengthen that of the domestic private sector but also of efforts that Member countries could take to provide markets for the exports expected from higher levels of foreign investors. It was also felt that the implementation of privatisation policies could open up some sectors and generate new flows of international direct investment. It was also noted that multinational initiatives could smooth the way for international direct investment.

With these encouraging results, a second Round Table was organised by the Export-Import Bank of Japan and the Committee in Tokyo in 1989 on "Foreign Direct Investment and the New Economic Environment". Again, the objectives were to pursue efforts to improve mutual understanding and to increase international direct investment in non-Member countries. After discussing the implications of recent trends in international direct investment, the Round Table focused particularly on means of promoting international direct investment in the heavily-indebted countries, and on the impact that the new technologies are likely to have on international direct investment in these countries.

Participants to the Round Table pointed out that the combined efforts of enterprises, international organisations and host and home country governments were required to increase international direct investment in non-Member countries. The role that the OECD Member countries have played in setting the pace and showing the way by abolishing restrictions on international direct investment was underlined; Member countries can boost the economies of the non-Member countries by maintaining an open investment climate and sustaining global economic growth and by increasing the volume of international capital flows accompanied by technology transfers. The importance of international direct investment for the heavily-indebted countries was also underlined, since such investment provides a non-debt creating source of external finance. The Round Table emphasised that non-Member countries that had been the most successful in attracting international direct investment were those that had implemented more open and more stable foreign investment régimes.

In June 1990, in co-operation with the OECD Centre for Co-operation with the European Economies in Transition, the Committee held a seminar on foreign direct investment issues in Central and Eastern Europe. The purpose of this seminar was to identify the areas and means by which the countries of the region could benefit from the experience, policy advice and practical assistance of the OECD in promoting higher flows of foreign direct investment and its contribution to structural reform. The meeting dealt with a broad range of issues relevant to the formulation and implementation of policies designed to increase the attractiveness of these countries to potential investors. Confronted by the need to modernise their economies in response to the deterioration of their economic situation, most of the countries of central and eastern Europe began to undertake policy reforms aimed at liberalising and restructuring their economies to improve the competitiveness of their industries. Participants were of the view that foreign direct investment can play an important role in the change from centrally planned to market economies and the restructuring of the economy that is crucial to the success of this transition.

Participants were also of the view that privatisation has now become an important element in the restructuring policies of the countries of the region, and that the success of privatisation programmes will be crucial in determining the effectiveness of efforts to restructure the enterprise sector. Foreign capital is considered as being essential to the privatisation programmes given the paucity of private domestic capital and the lack of domestic capital markets. The development of the services sector was viewed by participants as one of the major tasks ahead in the transformation and restructuring of the economies of Central and Eastern Europe.

As a result of the above developments, more countries will have to share responsibility for the international investment climate and many of these concern observing clear and equitable rules of the game. Within the overall framework of the Organisation's efforts in this area, the Committee will be examining, in the years ahead, how it may build on the dialogue that has commenced to promote further direct investment in the countries of Central and Eastern Europe, in the Dynamic Asian Economies and in Latin America countries, and the conditions necessary to this end.

NOTE

1. Brunei, Indonesia, Malaysia, Philippines, Singapore, Thailand.

DECLARATION ON INTERNATIONAL INVESTMENT AND MULTINATIONAL ENTERPRISES

(21 June 1976)

THE GOVERNMENTS OF OECD MEMBER COUNTRIES[1]

CONSIDERING:

- That international investment has assumed increased importance in the world economy and has considerably contributed to the development of their countries;
- That multinational enterprises play an important role in this investment process;
- That co-operation by Member countries can improve the foreign investment climate, encourage the positive contribution which multinational enterprises can make to economic and social progress, and minimise and resolve difficulties which may arise from their various operations;
- That, while continuing endeavours within the OECD may lead to further international arrangements and agreements in this field, it seems appropriate at this stage to intensify their co-operation and consultation on issues relating to international investment and multinational enterprises through inter-related instruments each of which deals with a different aspect of the matter and together constitute a framework within which the OECD will consider these issues;

DECLARE:

Guidelines for Multinational Enterprises	I.	That they jointly recommend to multinational enterprises operating in their territories the observance of the Guidelines as set forth in Annex 1 hereto having regard to the considerations and understandings which introduce the Guidelines and are an integral part of them;
National Treatment	II.1.	That Member countries should, consistent with their needs to maintain public order, to protect their essential security interests and to fulfil commitments relating to international peace and security, accord to enterprises operating in their territories and owned or controlled directly or indirectly by nationals of another Member country (hereinafter referred to as ''Foreign-Controlled Enterprises'') treatment under their laws, regulations and administrative practices, consistent with international law and no less favourable than that accorded in like situations to domestic enterprises (hereinafter referred to as ''National Treatment'');
	2.	That Member countries will consider applying ''national Treatment'' in respect of countries other than Member countries;

<table>
<tr><td></td><td>3.</td><td>That Member countries will endeavour to ensure that their territorial subdivisions apply "National Treatment";</td></tr>
<tr><td></td><td>4.</td><td>That this Declaration does not deal with the right of Member countries to regulate the entry of foreign investment or the conditions of establishment of foreign enterprises;</td></tr>
<tr><td>Conflicting Requirements</td><td>III.</td><td>That they will co-operate with a view to avoiding sor minimising the imposition of conflicting requirements on multinational enterprises and that they will take into account the general considerations and practical approaches as set forth in Annex 2 hereto.</td></tr>
<tr><td>International Investment Incentives and Disincentives</td><td>IV.1.</td><td>That they recognise the need to strengthen their co-operation in the field of international direct investment;</td></tr>
<tr><td></td><td>2.</td><td>That they thus recognise the need to give due weight to the interests of Member countries affected by specific laws, regulations and administrative practices in this field (hereinafter called "measures") providing official incentives and disincentives to international direct investment;</td></tr>
<tr><td></td><td>3.</td><td>That Member countries will endeavour to make such measures as transparent as possible, so that their importance and purpose can be ascertained and that information on them can be readily available;</td></tr>
<tr><td>Consultation Procedures</td><td>V.</td><td>That they are prepared to consult one another on the above matters in conformity with the Decisions of the Council on the Guidelines for Multinational Enterprises, on National Treatment and on International Investment Incentives and Disincentives;</td></tr>
<tr><td>Review</td><td>VI.</td><td>That they will review the above matters within three years with a view to improving the effectiveness of international economic co-operation among Member countries on issues relating to international investment and multinational enterprises[2].</td></tr>
</table>

GUIDELINES FOR MULTINATIONAL ENTERPRISES[3]

1.   Multinational enterprises now play an important part in the economies of Member countries and in international economic relations, which is of increasing interest to governments. Through international direct investment, such enterprises can bring substantial benefits to home and host countries by contributing to the efficient utilisation of capital, technology and human resources between countries and can thus fulfil an important role in the promotion of economic and social welfare. But the advances made by multinational enterprises in organising their operations beyond the national framework may lead to abuse of concentrations of economic power and to conflicts with national policy objectives. In addition, the complexity of these multinational enterprises and the difficulty of clearly perceiving their diverse structures, operations and policies sometimes give rise to concern.

2.   The common aim of the Member countries is to encourage the positive contributions which multinational enterprises can make to economic and social progress and to minimise and resolve the difficulties to which their various operations may give rise. In view of the transnational structure of such enterprises, this aim will be furthered by co-operation among the OECD countries where the headquarters of most of the multinational enterprises are established and which are the location of a substantial part of their operations. The Guidelines set out hereafter are designed to assist in the achievement of this common aim and to contribute to improving the foreign investment climate.

3.   Since the operations of multinational enterprises extend throughout the world, including countries that are not Members of the Organisation, international co-operation in this field should extend to all States. Member countries will give their full support to efforts undertaken in co-operation with non-member countries, and in particular with developing countries, with a view to improving the welfare and living standards of all people both by encouraging the positive contributions which multinational enterprises can make and by minimising and resolving the problems which may arise in connection with their activities.

4.   Within the Organisation, the programme of co-operation to attain these ends will be a continuing, pragmatic and balanced one. It comes within the general aims of the Convention on the Organisation for Economic Co-operation and Development (OECD) and makes full use of the various specialised bodies of the Organisation, whose terms of reference already cover many aspects of the role of multinational enterprises, notably in matters of international trade and payments, competition, taxation, manpower, industrial development, science and technology. In these bodies, work is being carried out on the identification of issues, the improvement of relevant qualitative and statistical information and the elaboration of proposals for action designed to strengthen inter-governmental co-operation. In some of these areas procedures already exist through which issues related to the operations of multinational enterprises can be taken up. This work could result in the conclusion of further and complementary agreements and arrangements between governments.

5. The initial phase of the co-operation programme is composed of a Declaration and three Decisions promulgated simultaneously as they are complementary and inter-connected, in respect of Guidelines for multinational enterprises, National Treatment for foreign-controlled enterprises and international investment incentives and disincentives.

6. The Guidelines set out below are recommendations jointly addressed by Member countries to multinational enterprises operating in their territories. These Guidelines, which take into account the problems which can arise because of the international structure of these enterprises, lay down standards for the activities of these enterprises in the different Member countries. Observance of the Guidelines is voluntary and not legally enforceable. However, they should help to ensure that the operations of these enterprises are in harmony with national policies of the countries where they operate and to strengthen the basis of mutual confidence between enterprises and States.

7. Every State has the right to prescribe the conditions under which multinational enterprises operate within its national jurisdiction, subject to international law and to the international agreements to which it has subscribed. The entities of a multinational enterprise located in various countries are subject to the laws of these countries.

8. A precise legal definition of multinational enterprises is not required for the purposes of the Guidelines. These usually comprise companies or other entities whose ownership is private, state or mixed, established in different countries and so linked that one or more of them may be able to exercise a significant influence over the activities of others and, in particular, to share knowledge and resources with the others. The degrees of autonomy of each entity in relation to the others varies widely from one multinational enterprise to another, depending on the nature of the links between such entities and the fields of activity concerned. For these reasons, the Guidelines are addressed to the various entities within the multinational enterprise (parent companies and/or local entities) according to the actual distribution of responsibilities among them on the understanding that they will co-operate and provide assistance to one another as necessary to facilitate observance of the Guidelines. The word ''enterprise'' as used in these Guidelines refers to these various entities in accordance with their responsibilities.

9. The Guidelines are not aimed at introducing differences of treatment between multinational and domestic enterprises; wherever relevant they reflect good practice for all. Accordingly, multinational and domestic enterprises are subject to the same expectations in respect of their conduct wherever the Guidelines are relevant to both.

10. The use of appropriate international dispute settlement mechanisms, including arbitration, should be encouraged as a means of facilitating the resolution of problems arising between enterprises and Member countries.

11. Member countries have agreed to establish appropriate review and consultation procedures concerning issues arising in respect of the Guidelines. When multinational enterprises are made subject to conflicting requirements by Member countries, the governments concerned will co-operate in good faith with a view to resolving such problems either within the Committee on International Investment and Multinational Enterprises established by the OECD Council on 21st January 1975 or through other mutually acceptable arrangements.

Having regard to the foregoing considerations, the Member countries set forth the following Guidelines for multinational enterprises with the understanding that Member countries will fulfil their responsibilities to treat enterprises equitably and in accordance with international law and international agreements as well as contractual obligations to which they have subscribed.

GENERAL POLICIES

Enterprises should:

    1. Take fully into account established general policy objectives of the Member countries in which they operate;

2. In particular, give due consideration to those countries' aims and priorities with regard to economic and social progress, including industrial and regional development, the protection of the environment and consumer interests, the creation of employment opportunities, the promotion of innovation and the transfer of technology[4];

3. While observing their legal obligations concerning information, supply their entities with supplementary information the latter may need in order to meet requests by the authorities of the countries in which those entities are located for information relevant to the activities of those entities, taking into account legitimate requirements of business confidentiality;

4. Favour close co-operation with the local community and business interests;

5. Allow their component entities freedom to develop their activities and to exploit their competitive advantage in domestic and foreign markets, consistent with the need for specialisation and sound commercial practice;

6. When filling responsible posts in each country of operation, take due account of individual qualifications without discrimination as to nationality, subject to particular national requirements in this respect;

7. Not render and they should not be solicited or expected to render any bribe or other improper benefit, direct or indirect, to any public servant or holder of public office;

8. Unless legally permissible, not make contributions to candidates for public office or to political parties or other political organisations;

9. Abstain from any improper involvement in local political activities.

DISCLOSURE OF INFORMATION

Enterprises should, having due regard to their nature and relative size in the economic context of their operations and to requirements of business confidentiality and to cost, publish in a form suited to improve public understanding a sufficient body of factual information on the structure, activities and policies of the enterprise as a whole, as a supplement, insofar as necessary for this purpose, to information to be disclosed under the national law of the individual countries in which they operate. To this end, they should publish within reasonable time limits, on a regular basis, but at least annually, financial statements and other pertinent information relating to the enterprise as a whole, comprising in particular:

a) The structure of the enterprise, showing the name and location of the parent company, its main affiliates, its percentage ownership, direct and indirect, in these affiliates, including shareholdings between them;

b) The geographical areas[5] where operations are carried out and the principal activities carried on therein by the parent company and the main affiliates;

c) The operating results and sales by geographical area and the sales in the major line of business for the enterprise as a whole;

d) Significant new capital investment by geographical area and, as far as practicable, by major lines of business for the enterprise as a whole;

e) A statement of the sources and uses of funds by the enterprise as a whole;

f) The average number of employees in each geographical area;

g) Research and development expenditure for the enterprise as a whole;

h) The policies followed in respect of intra-group pricing;

i) The accounting policies, including those on consolidation, observed in compiling the published information.

COMPETITION

Enterprises should, while conforming to official competition rules and established policies of the countries in which they operate.

1. Refrain from actions which would adversely affect competition in the relevant market by abusing a dominant position of market power, by means of, for example:
   a) Anti-competitive acquisitions;
   b) Predatory behaviour toward competitors;
   c) Unreasonable refusal to deal;
   d) Anti-competitive abuse of industrial property rights;
   e) Discriminatory (i.e. unreasonably differentiated) pricing and using such pricing transactions between affiliated enterprises as a means of affecting adversely competition outside these enterprises;
2. Allow purchasers, distributors and licensees freedom to resell, export, purchase and develop their operations consistent with law, trade conditions, the need for specialisation and sound commercial practice;
3. Refrain from participating in or otherwise purposely strengthening the restrictive effects of international or domestic cartels or restrictive agreements which adversely affect or eliminate competition and which are not generally or specifically accepted under applicable national or international legislation;
4. Be ready to consult and co-operate, including the provision of information, with competent authorities of countries whose interests are directly affected in regard to competition issues or investigations. Provisions of information should be in accordance with safeguards normally applicable in this field.

FINANCING

Enterprises should, in managing the financial and commercial operations of their activities, and especially their liquid foreign assets and liabilities, take into consideration the established objectives of the countries in which they operate regarding balance of payments and credit policies.

TAXATION

Enterprises should:

1. Upon request of the taxation authorities of the countries in which they operate provide, in accordance with the safeguards and relevant procedures of the national laws of these countries, the information necessary to determine correctly the taxes to be assessed in connection with their operations, including relevant information concerning their operations in other countries;
2. Refrain from making use of the particular facilities available to them, such as transfer pricing which does not conform to an arm's length standard, for modifying in ways contrary to national laws the tax base on which members of the group are assessed.

EMPLOYMENT AND INDUSTRIAL RELATIONS

Enterprises should, within the framework of law, regulations and prevailing labour relations and employment practices, in each of the countries in which they operate:

106

1. Respect the right of their employees to be represented by trade unions and other bona fide organisations of employees, and engage in constructive negotiations, either individually or through employers' associations, with such employee organisations with a view to reaching agreements on employment conditions, which should include provisions for dealing with disputes arising over the interpretation of such agreements, and for ensuring mutually respected rights and responsibilities;
2. *a)* Provide such facilities to representatives of the employees as may be necessary to assist in the development of effective collective agreements;
   b) Provide to representatives of employees information which is needed for meaningful negotiations on conditions of employment;
3. Provide to representatives of employees where this accords with local law and practice, information which enables them to obtain a true and fair view of the performance of the entity or, where appropriate, the enterprise as a whole;
4. Observe standards of employment and industrial relations not less favourable than those observed by comparable employers in the host country;
5. In their operations, to the greatest extent practicable, utilise, train and prepare for upgrading members of the local labour force in co-operation with representatives of their employees and, where appropriate, the relevant governmental authorities;
6. In considering changes in their operations which would have major effects upon the livelihood of their employees, in particular in the case of the closure of an entity involving collective lay-offs or dismissals, provide reasonable notice of such changes to representatives of their employees, and where appropriate to the relevant governmental authorities and co-operate with the employee representatives and appropriate governmental authorities so as to mitigate to the maximum extent practicable adverse effects;
7. Implement their employment policies including hiring, discharge, pay, promotion and training without discrimination unless selectivity in respect of employee characteristics is in furtherance of established governmental policies which specifically promote greater equality of employment opportunity;
8. In the context of bona fide negotiations[6] with representatives of employees on conditions of employment, or while employees are exercising a right to organise, not threaten to utilise a capacity to transfer the whole or part of an operating unit from the country concerned nor transfer employees from the enterprises' component entities in other countries in order to influence unfairly those negotiations or to hinder the exercise of a right to organise;[7]
9. Enable authorised representatives of their employees to conduct negotiations on collective bargaining or labour management relations issues with representatives of management who are authorised to take decisions on the matters under negotiation.

ENVIRONMENTAL PROTECTION[8]

Enterprises should, within the framework of laws, regulations and administrative practices in the countries in which they operate, and recalling the provisions of paragraph 9 of the Introduction to the Guidelines that, inter alia, multinational and domestic enterprises are subject to the same expectations in respect of their conduct whenever the Guidelines are relevant to both, take due account of the need to protect the environment and avoid creating environmentally related health problems. In particular, enterprises, whether multinational or domestic, should:

1. Assess, and take into account in decision making, foreseeable environmental and environmentally related health consequences of their activities, including citing decisions, impact on indigenous natural resources and foreseeable environmental and environmentally related health risks of products as well as from the generation, transport and disposal of waste;
2. Co-operate with competent authorities, inter alia, by providing adequate and timely information regarding the potential impacts on the environment and environmentally related

health aspects of all their activities and by providing the relevant expertise available in the enterprise as a whole;

3. Take appropriate measures in their operations to minimise the risk of accidents and damage to health and the environment, and to co-operate in mitigating adverse effects, in particular:

    a) by selecting and adopting those technologies and practices which are compatible with these objectives;

    b) by introducing a system of environmental protection at the level of the enterprise as a whole including, where appropriate, the use of environmental auditing;

    c) by enabling their component entities to be adequately equipped, especially by providing them with adequate knowledge and assistance;

    d) by implementing education and training programmes for their employees;

    e) by preparing contingency plans; and

    f) by supporting, in an appropriate manner, public information and community awareness programmes.

SCIENCE AND TECHNOLOGY

Enterprises should:

1. Endeavour to ensure that their activities fit satisfactorily into the scientific and technological policies and plans of the countries in which they operate, and contribute to the development of national scientific and technological capacities, including as far as appropriate the establishment and improvement in host countries of their capacity to innovate;

2. To the fullest extent practicable, adopt in the course of their business activities practices which permit the rapid diffusion of technologies with due regard to the protection of industrial and intellectual property rights;

3. When granting licenses for the use of industrial property rights or when otherwise transferring technology, do so on reasonable terms and conditions.

Annex 2

GENERAL CONSIDERATIONS AND PRACTICAL APPROACHES CONCERNING CONFLICTING REQUIREMENTS IMPOSED ON MULTINATIONAL ENTERPRISES[9]

GENERAL CONSIDERATIONS

1.   In contemplating new legislation, action under existing legislation or other exercise of juris-diction which may conflict with the legal requirements or established policies of another Member country and lead to conflicting requirements being imposed on multinational enterprises, the Member countries concerned should:

  a) Have regard to relevant principles of international law;
  b) Endeavour to avoid or minimise such conflicts and the problems to which they give rise by following an approach of moderation and restraint, respecting and accommodating the interests of other Member countries[10];
  c) Take fully into account the sovereignty and legitimate economic, law enforcement and other interests of other Member countries;
  d) Bear in mind the importance of permitting the observance of contractual obligations and the possible adverse impact of measures having a retroactive effect.

2.   Member countries should endeavour to promote co-operation as an alternative to unilateral action to avoid or minimise conflicting requirements and problems arising therefrom. Member countries should on request consult one another and endeavour to arrive at mutually acceptable solutions to such problems.

PRACTICAL APPROACHES

3.   Member countries recognised that in the majority of circumstances, effective co-operation may best be pursued on a bilateral basis. On the other hand, there may be cases where the multilateral approach could be more effective.

4.   Member countries should therefore be prepared to:

  a) Develop mutually beneficial, practical and appropriately safeguarded bilateral arrange-ments, formal or informal, for notification to and consultation with other Member countries;
  b) Give prompt and sympathetic consideration to requests for notification and bilateral consultation on an ad hoc basis made by any Member country which considers that its interests may be affected by a measure of the type referred to under paragraph 1 above, taken by another Member country with which it does not have such bilateral arrangements;
  c) Inform the other concerned Member countries as soon as practicable of new legislation or regulations proposed by their Governments for adoption which have significant potential

for conflict with the legal requirements or established policies of other Member countries and for giving rise to conflicting requirements being imposed on multinational enterprises;

d) Give prompt and sympathetic consideration to requests by other Member countries for consultation in the Committee on International Investment and Multinational Enterprises or through other mutually acceptable arrangements. Such consultations would be facilitated by notification at the earliest stage practicable;

e) Give prompt and full consideration to proposals which may be made by other Member countries in any such consultations that would lessen or eliminate conflicts.

These procedures do not apply to those aspects of restrictive business practices or other matters which are the subject of existing OECD arrangements.

NOTES AND REFERENCES

1. On matters falling within its competence, the European Economic Community is associated with the section on National Treatment.

2. The Declaration was reviewed in 1979, 1984 and 1991. Section III on Conflicting Requirements was added following the 1991 Review.

3. The Guidelines were reviewed in 1979, 1984 and 1991. These reviews resulted in modification of the General Policies chapter (paragraph 2); the Disclosure of Information chapter [sub-paragraph b)]; a clarification and modification of the Employment and Industrial Relations chapter (paragraph 8); and the addition of a new chapter on the Environment.

4. This paragraph includes the additional provision concerning consumer interests, adopted by the OECD Governments at the meeting of the OECD Council at Ministerial level on 17 and 18 May 1984.

* 5. *For the purposes of the Guideline on Disclosure of Information the term "geographical area" means groups of countries or individual countries as each enterprise determines is appropriate in its particular circumstances. While no single method of grouping is appropriate for all enterprises or for all purposes, the factors to be considered by an enterprise would include the significance of geographic proximity, economic affinity, similarities in business environments and the nature, scale and degree of interrelationship of the enterprises' operations in the various countries.*

* 6. *Bona fide negotiations may include labour disputes as part of the process of negotiation. Whether or not labour disputes are so included will be determined by the law and prevailing employment practices of particular countries.*

7. This paragraph includes the additional provision, concerning transfer of employees, adopted by OECD Governments at the meeting of the OECD Council at Ministerial level on 13 and 14 June 1979.

8. This chapter was added at the meeting of the OECD Council at Ministerial level on 4 and 5 June 1991.

9. The General Considerations and Practical Approaches were endorsed by the Ministers in May 1984. They were annexed to the 1976 Declaration as a result of the 1991 Review exercise.

*10. *Applying the principle of comity, as it is understood in some Member countries, includes following an approach of this nature in exercising one's jurisdiction.*

---

* These texts are integral parts of the negotiated instruments.

Annex II

PROCEDURAL DECISIONS OF THE OECD COUNCIL

1. NATIONAL TREATMENT:
THIRD REVISED DECISION OF THE COUNCIL

December 1991

THE COUNCIL,

Having regard to the Convention on the Organisation for Economic Co-operation and Development of 14th December 1960 and, in particular, to Articles 2*c)*, 2*d)*, 3 and 5*a)* there of;

Having regard to the Resolution of the Council of 13th December 1984 on the Terms of Reference of the Committee on International Investment and Multinational Enterprises [C(84)171(Final)];

Having regard to the Section on National Treatment of the Declaration by Governments of OECD Member countries of 21st June 1976 on International Investment and Multinational Enterprises [hereinafter called "the Declaration"];

Having regard to the Second Revised Decision of the Council of 17th May 1984 on National Treatment [C(84)91];

Having regard to the report on the National Treatment Instrument by the Committee on International Investment and Multinational Enterprises [C(91)147 and Corrigendum 1];

Considering it appropriate to strengthen the procedures established within the Organisation for reviewing laws, regulations and administrative practices (hereinafter called "measures") which depart from National Treatment, as defined in the Declaration (hereinafter called "National Treatment");

On the proposal of the Committee on International Investment and Multinational Enterprises;

DECIDES:

The Second Revised Decision of the Council of 17th May 1984 on National Treatment [C(84)91] is repealed and replaced by the following:

Article 1

NOTIFICATION

a) Members[1] shall notify the Organisation of all measures constituting exceptions to National Treatment within 60 days of their adoption and of any other measures which have a bearing on National Treatment. All exceptions shall be set out in Annex A to this Decision[2].

b) Members shall notify the Organisation within 60 days of their introduction of any modifications of the measures covered in paragraph *a)*.

c) The Organisation shall consider the notifications submitted to it in accordance with the provisions of paragraphs *a)* and *b)* with a view to determining whether each Member is meeting its commitments under the Declaration.

Article 2

EXAMINATION

a) The Organisation shall examine each exception lodged by a Member and other measures notified under Article 1 at intervals to be determined by the Organisation. These intervals shall, however, be not more than three years, unless the Council decides otherwise.

b) Each Member shall notify the Organisation prior to the periodic examination called for in paragraph *a)*, whether it desires to maintain any exception lodged by it under Article 1 and if so, state its reasons therefore.

c) The examinations provided for in paragraph *a)* shall be directed at making suitable proposals designed to assist Members to withdraw their exceptions.

d) The examinations provided for in paragraph *a)* shall be country reviews in which all of the exceptions lodged by a Member are covered in the same examination.

e) Notwithstanding paragraph *d)*, the examinations provided for in paragraph *a)* may focus on specific types or groups of measures of particular concern, as and when determined by the Organisation.

Article 3

REFERENCE TO THE ORGANISATION

a) If a Member considers that another Member has, contrary to its undertakings with regard to National Treatment, retained, introduced or reintroduced measures and if it considers itself to be prejudiced thereby, it may refer to the Organisation.

b) The fact that the case is under consideration by the Organisation shall not preclude the Member which has referred to the Organisation from entering into bilateral discussion on the matter with the other Member concerned.

Article 4

COMMITTEE ON INTERNATIONAL INVESTMENT
AND MULTINATIONAL ENTERPRISES: GENERAL TASKS

a) The Committee on International Investment and Multinational Enterprises (hereinafter called "the Committee") shall consider all questions concerning the interpretation or implementation of the provisions of the Declaration or of Acts of the Council relating to National Treatment and shall report its conclusions thereon to the Council.

b) The Committee shall submit to the Council any appropriate proposals in connection with its tasks as defined in paragraph a) and, in particular, with the abolishing of measures constituting exceptions to National Treatment.

Article 5

COMMITTEE ON INTERNATIONAL INVESTMENT
AND MULTINATIONAL ENTERPRISES: SPECIAL TASKS

a) The Committee shall:
   i) consider, in conformity with paragraphs a) and b) of Article 2, each exception notified to the Organisation and make, where appropriate, suitable proposals to assist Members to withdraw their exceptions;
   ii) consider, in accordance with Article 1, the notifications submitted to the Organisation;
   iii) consider references submitted to the Organisation in accordance with the provisions of Article 3;
   iv) act as a forum for consultations, at the request of a Member, in respect of any matter related to the Declaration and its implementation.

b) The Committee may periodically invite the Business and Industry Advisory Committee to the OECD (BIAC) and the Trade Union Advisory Committee to the OECD (TUAC) to express their views on matters related to National Treatment and shall take account of such views in its reports to the Council.

Article 6

REVIEW OF THE DECISION

This Decision shall be reviewed within three years.

Article 7

PARTICIPATION BY THE EUROPEAN ECONOMIC COMMUNITY

The present Decision, as well as any further Decision amending it, shall be open for accession by the European Economic Community. Such accession shall be notified to the Secretary-General of the Organisation.

2. THE GUIDELINES FOR MULTINATIONAL ENTERPRISES: SECOND REVISED DECISION OF THE COUNCIL

Amended June 1991

THE COUNCIL,

Having regard to the Convention on the Organisation for Economic Co-operation and Development of 14th December 1960 and, in particular, to Articles 2d), 3 and 5a) there of;

Having regard to the Resolution of the Council of 28th November 1979, on the Terms of Reference of the Committee on International Investment and Multinational Enterprises and, in particular, to paragraph 2 thereof [C(79)210(Final)];

Taking note of the Declaration by the Governments of OECD Member countries of 21st June 1976 in which they jointly recommend to multinational enterprises the observance of Guidelines for multinational enterprises;

Having regard to the Revised Decision of the Council of 13th June 1979 on Inter-Governmental Consultation Procedures on the Guidelines for Multinational Enterprises [C(79)143(Final)];

Recognising the desirability of setting forth procedures by which consultations may take place on matters related to these Guidelines;

Recognising that, while bilateral and multilateral co-operation should be strengthened when multinational enterprises are made subject to conflicting requirements, effective co-operation on problems arising therefrom may best be pursued in most circumstances on a bilateral level, although there may be cases where the multilateral approach would be more effective;

Considering the Report on the Review of the 1976 Declaration and Decisions on International Investment and Multinational Enterprises [C(79)102(Final)] and the Report on the Second Review of the 1976 Declaration and Decisions on International Investment and Multinational Enterprises [C/MIN(84)5(Final)], including the particular endorsement of the section in the Second Review Report relating to conflicting requirements;

On the proposal of the Committee on International Investment and Multinational Enterprises:

DECIDES:

1.   Member Governments shall set up National Contact Points for undertaking promotional activities, handling inquires and for discussions with the parties concerned on all matters related to the Guidelines so that they can contribute to the solution of problems which may arise in this connection. The business community, employee organisations and other interested parties shall be informed of the availability of such facilities.

2.   National Contact Points in different countries shall co-operate if such need arises, on any matter related to the Guidelines relevant to their activities. As a general procedure, discussions at the national level should be initiated before contacts with other National Contact Points are undertaken.

3.   The Committee on International Investment and Multinational Enterprises (hereinafter called "the Committee") shall periodically or at the request of a Member country hold an exchange of views on matters related to the Guidelines and the experience gained in their application. The Committee shall be responsible for clarification of the Guidelines. Clarification will be provided as required. The Committee shall periodically report to the Council on these matters.

4.   The Committee shall periodically invite the Business and Industry Advisory Committee to OECD (BIAC) and the Trade Union Advisory Committee to OECD (TUAC) to express their views on matters related to the Guidelines. In addition, exchanges of views with the advisory bodies on

these matters may be held upon request by the latter. The Committee shall take account of such views in its reports to the Council.

5.   If it so wishes, an individual enterprise will be given the opportunity to express its views either orally or in writing on issues concerning the Guidelines involving its interests.

6.   The Committee shall not reach conclusions on the conduct of individual enterprises.

7.   This Decision shall be reviewed at the latest in six years. The Committee shall make proposals for this purpose as appropriate.

8.   This Decision shall replace Decision [C(79)143].

3. INTERNATIONAL INVESTMENT INCENTIVES AND DISINCENTIVES: SECOND REVISED DECISION OF THE COUNCIL

May 1984

THE COUNCIL,

Having regard to the Convention on the Organisation for Economic Co-operation and Development of 14th December 1960 and, in particular, Articles 2c), 2d), 2e), 3 and 5a) there of;

Having regard to the Resolution of the Council of 28th November 1979 on the Terms of Reference of the Committee on International Investment and Multinational Enterprises [C(79)210(Final)];

Taking note of the Declaration by the Governments of OECD Member countries of 21st June 1976 on International Investment Incentives and Disincentives;

Having regard to the Revised Decision of the Council of 13th June 1979 on International Investment Incentives and Disincentives [C(79)145];

Considering the Report on the Second Review of the 1976 Declaration and Decisions on International Investment and Multinational Enterprises [C/MIN(84)5(Final)];

On the proposal of the Committee on International Investment and Multinational Enterprises;

DECIDES:

1. Consultations will take place in the framework of the Committee on International Investment and Multinational Enterprises at the request of a Member country which considers that its interests may be adversely affected by the impact on its flow of international direct investments of measures taken by another Member country which provide significant official incentives and disincentives to international direct investment. Having full regard to the national economic objectives of the measures and without prejudice to policies designed to redress regional imbalances, the purpose of the consultations will be to examine the possibility of reducing such effects to a minimum.

2. Member countries shall supply, under the consultation procedures, all permissible information relating to any measures being the subject of the consultation.

3. The Committee may periodically invite the Business and Industry Advisory Committee to OECD (BIAC) and the Trade Union Advisory Committee to OECD (TUAC) to express their views on matters relating to international investment incentives and disincentives and shall take account of these views in its periodic reports to the Council.

4. This Decision shall be reviewed at the latest in six years. The Committee on International Investment and Multinational Enterprises shall make proposals for this purpose as appropriate.

5. This Decision shall replace Decision [C(79)145].

4. CONFLICTING REQUIREMENTS: DECISION OF THE COUNCIL

June 1991

THE COUNCIL,

Having regard to the Convention on the Organisation for Economic Co-operation and Development of 14th December 1960 and, in particular, to Articles 2*d)*, 3 and 5*a)* there of;

Having regard to the Resolution of the Council of 28th November 1979, on the Terms of Reference of the Committee on International Investment and Multinational Enterprises and, in particular, to paragraph 2 thereof [C(70)210(Final)];

Recalling that the Council at Ministerial level endorsed the Conclusions and Recommendations of the Report on the Second Review of the 1976 Declaration and Decisions on International Investment and Multinational Enterprises [C/MIN(84)5(Final)], and in particular the section in that Report on conflicting requirements;

Taking note of the Declaration by the Governments of OECD Member countries of 21st June 1976 (Revised 4-5 June 1991) in which they jointly recommend to Member countries to co-operate with a view of avoiding or minimising conflicting requirements being imposed on multinational enterprises;

Recognising the desirability of maintaining procedures by which consultations may take place on matters related to conflicting requirements;

Recognising that, while bilateral and multilateral co-operation should be strengthened when multinational enterprises are made subject to conflicting requirements, effective co-operation on problems arising therefrom may best be pursued in most circumstances on a bilateral level, although there may be cases where the multilateral approach would be more effective;

On the proposal of the Committee on International Investment and Multinational Enterprises:

DECIDES:

1.　Member countries may request that consultations be held in the Committee on any problem arising from the fact that multinational enterprises are made subject to conflicting requirements. The Member countries concerned shall give prompt and sympathetic consideration to requests by Member countries for consultations in the Committee or through other mutually acceptable arrangements, it being understood that such consultations would be facilitated by notification at the earliest stage practicable. Member countries concerned will co-operate in good faith with a view to resolving such problems, either within the Committee or through other mutually acceptable arrangements.

2.　The Committee will continue to serve as a forum for consideration of the question of conflicting requirements, including, as appropriate, the national and international legal principles involved.

3.　Member countries shall assist the Committee in its periodic reviews of experience on matters relating to conflicting requirements.

4.　The Committee shall periodically invite the Business and Industry Advisory Committee to the OECD (BIAC) and the Trade Union Advisory Committee to the OECD (TUAC) to express their views on matters relating to conflicting requirements.

5.　This Decision shall be reviewed at the latest in 1997. The Committee shall make proposals for this purpose as appropriate.

6.   Paragraphs 7 to 10 of the Decision on the Guidelines for Multinational Enterprises [C(84)90] are repealed.

NOTES AND REFERENCES

*1.   *For the purposes of this Decision, "Members" means all parties to the Decision.*

2.   In the interests of brevity, Annex A to the Decision is not reproduced herein. A forthcoming publication on National Treatment for Established Foreign-Controlled Enterprises will reproduce the list of country exceptions in its entirety.

---

* This text in an integral part of the negotiated instrument.

MAIN SALES OUTLETS OF OECD PUBLICATIONS – PRINCIPAUX POINTS DE VENTE DES PUBLICATIONS DE L'OCDE

Argentina – Argentine
Carlos Hirsch S.R.L.
Galería Güemes, Florida 165, 4° Piso
1333 Buenos Aires   Tel. (1) 331.1787 y 331.2391
                                      Telefax: (1) 331.1787

Australia – Australie
D.A. Book (Aust.) Pty. Ltd.
648 Whitehorse Road, P.O.B 163
Mitcham, Victoria 3132   Tel. (03) 873.4411
                                          Telefax: (03) 873.5679

Austria – Autriche
OECD Publications and Information Centre
Schedestrasse 7
D-W 5300 Bonn 1 (Germany)   Tel. (49.228) 21.60.45
                                          Telefax: (49.228) 26.11.04

Gerold & Co.
Graben 31
Wien I   Tel. (0222) 533.50.14

Belgium – Belgique
Jean De Lannoy
Avenue du Roi 202
B-1060 Bruxelles   Tel. (02) 538.51.69/538.08.41
                            Telefax: (02) 538.08.41

Canada
Renouf Publishing Company Ltd.
1294 Algoma Road
Ottawa, ON K1B 3W8   Tel. (613) 741.4333
                                      Telefax: (613) 741.5439
Stores:
61 Sparks Street
Ottawa, ON K1P 5R1   Tel. (613) 238.8985
211 Yonge Street
Toronto, ON M5B 1M4   Tel. (416) 363.3171
Federal Publications
165 University Avenue
Toronto, ON M5H 3B8   Tel. (416) 581.1552
                                      Telefax: (416)581.1743
Les Éditions La Liberté Inc.
3020 Chemin Sainte-Foy
Sainte-Foy, PQ G1X 3V6   Tel. (418) 658.3763
                                          Telefax: (418) 658.3763

China – Chine
China National Publications Import
 Export Corporation (CNPIEC)
P.O. Box 88
Beijing   Tel. 44.0731
                                Telefax: 401.5661

Denmark – Danemark
Munksgaard Export and Subscription Service
35, Nørre Søgade, P.O. Box 2148
DK-1016 København K   Tel. (33) 12.85.70
                                      Telefax: (33) 12.93.87

Finland – Finlande
Akateeminen Kirjakauppa
Keskuskatu 1, P.O. Box 128
00100 Helsinki   Tel. (358 0) 12141
                              Telefax: (358 0) 121.4441

France
OECD/OCDE
Mail Orders/Commandes par correspondance:
2, rue André-Pascal
75775 Paris Cédex 16   Tel. (33-1) 45.24.82.00
                                  Telefax: (33-1) 45.24.85.00
                                  or (33-1) 45.24.81.76
                                  Telex: 620 160 OCDE
Bookshop/Librairie:
33, rue Octave-Feuillet
75016 Paris   Tel. (33-1) 45.24.81.67
                              (33-1) 45.24.81.81
Librairie de l'Université
12a, rue Nazareth
13100 Aix-en-Provence   Tel. 42.26.18.08
                                          Telefax: 42.26.63.26

Germany – Allemagne
OECD Publications and Information Centre
Schedestrasse 7
D-W 5300 Bonn 1   Tel. (0228) 21.60.45
                              Telefax: (0228) 26.11.04

Greece – Grèce
Librairie Kauffmann
Mavrokordatou 9
106 78 Athens   Tel. 322.21.60
                            Telefax: 363.39.67

Hong Kong
Swindon Book Co. Ltd.
13 - 15 Lock Road
Kowloon, Hong Kong   Tel. 366.80.31
                                      Telefax: 739.49.75

Iceland – Islande
Mál Mog Menning
Laugavegi 18, Pósthólf 392
121 Reykjavik   Tel. 162.35.23

India – Inde
Oxford Book and Stationery Co.
Scindia House
New Delhi 110001   Tel.(11) 331.5896/5308
                                      Telefax: (11) 332.5993
17 Park Street
Calcutta 700016   Tel. 240832

Indonesia – Indonésie
Pdii-Lipi
P.O. Box 269/JKSMG/88
Jakarta 12790   Tel. 583467
                            Telex: 62 875

Ireland – Irlande
TDC Publishers – Library Suppliers
12 North Frederick Street
Dublin 1   Tel. 74.48.35/74.96.77
                        Telefax: 74.84.16

Israel
Electronic Publications only
Publications électroniques seulement
Sophist Systems Ltd.
71 Allenby Street
Tel-Aviv 65134   Tel. 3-29.00.21
                                  Telefax: 3-29.92.39

Italy – Italie
Libreria Commissionaria Sansoni
Via Duca di Calabria 1/1
50125 Firenze   Tel. (055) 64.54.15
                            Telefax: (055) 64.12.57
Via Bartolini 29
20155 Milano   Tel. (02) 36.50.83
Editrice e Libreria Herder
Piazza Montecitorio 120
00186 Roma   Tel. 679.46.28
                          Telex: NATEL I 621427
Libreria Hoepli
Via Hoepli 5
20121 Milano   Tel. (02) 86.54.46
                            Telefax: (02) 805.28.86
Libreria Scientifica
Dott. Lucio de Biasio 'Aeiou'
Via Meravigli 16
20123 Milano   Tel. (02) 805.68.98
                            Telefax: (02) 80.01.75

Japan – Japon
OECD Publications and Information Centre
Landic Akasaka Building
2-3-4 Akasaka, Minato-ku
Tokyo 107   Tel. (81.3) 3586.2016
                        Telefax: (81.3) 3584.7929

Korea – Corée
Kyobo Book Centre Co. Ltd.
P.O. Box 1658, Kwang Hwa Moon
Seoul   Tel. 730.78.91
                    Telefax: 735.00.30

Malaysia – Malaisie
Co-operative Bookshop Ltd.
University of Malaya
P.O. Box 1127, Jalan Pantai Baru
59700 Kuala Lumpur
Malaysia   Tel. 756.5000/756.5425
                        Telefax: 757.3661

Netherlands – Pays-Bas
SDU Uitgeverij
Christoffel Plantijnstraat 2
Postbus 20014
2500 EA's-Gravenhage   Tel. (070 3) 78.99.11
Voor bestellingen: Tel. (070 3) 78.98.80
                                  Telefax: (070 3) 47.63.51

New Zealand – Nouvelle-Zélande
GP Publications Ltd.
Customer Services
33 The Esplanade - P.O. Box 38-900
Petone, Wellington   Tel. (04) 5685.555
                                      Telefax: (04) 5685.333

Norway – Norvège
Narvesen Info Center - NIC
Bertrand Narvesens vei 2
P.O. Box 6125 Etterstad
0602 Oslo 6   Tel. (02) 57.33.00
                          Telefax: (02) 68.19.01

Pakistan
Mirza Book Agency
65 Shahrah Quaid-E-Azam
Lahore 3   Tel. 66.839
                        Telex: 44886 UBL PK. Attn: MIRZA BK

Portugal
Livraria Portugal
Rua do Carmo 70-74
Apart. 2681
1117 Lisboa Codex   Tel.: (01) 347.49.82/3/4/5
                                      Telefax: (01) 347.02.64

Singapore – Singapour
Information Publications Pte. Ltd.
Pei-Fu Industrial Building
24 New Industrial Road No. 02-06
Singapore 1953   Tel. 283.1786/283.1798
                                  Telefax: 284.8875

Spain – Espagne
Mundi-Prensa Libros S.A.
Castelló 37, Apartado 1223
Madrid 28001   Tel. (91) 431.33.99
                            Telefax: (91) 575.39.98
Libreria Internacional AEDOS
Consejo de Ciento 391
08009 - Barcelona   Tel. (93) 488.34.92
                                      Telefax: (93) 487.76.59
Llibreria de la Generalitat
Palau Moja
Rambla dels Estudis, 118
08002 - Barcelona   Tel. (93) 318.80.12 (Subscripcions)
                              (93) 302.67.23 (Publicacions)
                              Telefax: (93) 412.18.54

Sri Lanka
Centre for Policy Research
c/o Colombo Agencies Ltd.
No. 300-304, Galle Road
Colombo 3   Tel. (1) 574240, 573551-2
                        Telefax: (1) 575394, 510711

Sweden – Suède
Fritzes Fackboksföretaget
Box 16356
Regeringsgatan 12
103 27 Stockholm   Tel. (08) 23.89.00
                                      Telefax: (08) 20.50.21
Subscription Agency/Abonnements:
Wennergren-Williams AB
Nordenflychtsvägen 74
Box 30004
104 25 Stockholm   Tel. (08) 13.67.00
                                      Telefax: (08) 618.62.32

Switzerland – Suisse
OECD Publications and Information Centre
Schedestrasse 7
D-W 5300 Bonn 1 (Germany)   Tel. (49.228) 21.60.45
                                          Telefax: (49.228) 26.11.04
Suisse romande
Maditec S.A.
Chemin des Palettes 4
1020 Renens/Lausanne   Tel. (021) 635.08.65
                                          Telefax: (021) 635.07.80
Librairie Payot
6 rue Grenus
1211 Genève 11   Tel. (022) 731.89.50
                                Telex: 28356
Subscription Agency – Service des Abonnements
Naville S.A.
7, rue Lévrier
1201 Genève   Tél.: (022) 732.24.00
                            Telefax: (022) 738.87.13

Taiwan – Formose
Good Faith Worldwide Int'l. Co. Ltd.
9th Floor, No. 118, Sec. 2
Chung Hsiao E. Road
Taipei   Tel. (02) 391.7396/391.7397
                    Telefax: (02) 394.9176

Thailand – Thaïlande
Suksit Siam Co. Ltd.
113, 115 Fuang Nakhon Rd.
Opp. Wat Rajbopith
Bangkok 10200   Tel. (662) 251.1630
                                Telefax: (662) 236.7783

Turkey – Turquie
Kültur Yayinlari Is-Türk Ltd. Sti.
Atatürk Bulvari No. 191/Kat. 21
Kavaklidere/Ankara   Tel. 25.07.60
Dolmabahce Cad. No. 29
Besiktas/Istanbul   Tel. 160.71.88
                                Telex: 43482B

United Kingdom – Royaume-Uni
HMSO
Gen. enquiries   Tel. (071) 873 0011
Postal orders only:
P.O. Box 276, London SW8 5DT
Personal Callers HMSO Bookshop
49 High Holborn, London WC1V 6HB
                                Telefax: 071 873 2000
Branches at: Belfast, Birmingham, Bristol, Edinburgh,
                                                    Manchester

United States – États-Unis
OECD Publications and Information Centre
2001 L Street N.W., Suite 700
Washington, D.C. 20036-4910   Tel. (202) 785.6323
                                                  Telefax: (202) 785.0350

Venezuela
Libreria del Este
Avda F. Miranda 52, Aptdo. 60337
Edificio Galipán
Caracas 106   Tel. 951.1705/951.2307/951.1297
                            Telegram: Libreste Caracas

Yugoslavia – Yougoslavie
Jugoslovenska Knjiga
Knez Mihajlova 2, P.O. Box 36
Beograd   Tel. (011) 621.992
                        Telefax: (011) 625.970

Orders and inquiries from countries where Distributors have
not yet been appointed should be sent to: OECD Publications Service, 2 rue André-Pascal, 75775 Paris Cédex 16,
France.

Les commandes provenant de pays où l'OCDE n'a pas
encore désigné de distributeur devraient être adressées à :
OCDE, Service des Publications, 2, rue André-Pascal, 75775
Paris Cédex 16, France.

OECD PUBLICATIONS, 2 rue André-Pascal, 75775 PARIS CEDEX 16
PRINTED IN FRANCE
(21 92 02 1) ISBN 92-64-13629-0 - No. 45923 1992